MATT & SARAH ___RS

7

SE___N

___R___WS

___EK DEVOTIONAL *for Teens*

LifeWay Press
Nashville, Tennessee

© 2017 LifeWay Press®
Reprinted May 2018, Aug. 2018, Aug. 2019

No part of this work may be reproduced or transmitted in any form or
by any means, electronic or mechanical, including photocopying and
recording, or by any information storage or retrieval system, except as may
be expressly permitted in writing by the publisher.

Requests for permission should be addressed in writing to
LifeWay Press®, One LifeWay Plaza, Nashville, TN 37234.

ISBN: 978-1-4627-7755-6
Item Number: 005799056

Dewey Decimal Classification Number: 242.2
Subject Heading: DEVOTIONAL LITERATURE /
BIBLE STUDY AND TEACHING / GOD

Printed in the United States of America

Student Ministry Publishing
LifeWay Resources
One LifeWay Plaza
Nashville, TN 37234

We believe that the Bible has God for its author; salvation for its end; and
truth, without any mixture of error, for its matter and that all Scripture is
totally true and trustworthy. To review LifeWay's doctrinal guideline,
please visit www.lifeway.com/doctrinalguideline.

Unless otherwise noted, all Scripture quotations are taken from the
Christian Standard Bible®, Copyright © 2017 by Holman Bible Publishers.
Used by permission. Christian Standard Bible® and CSB® are federally
registered trademarks of Holman Bible Publishers.

TABLE OF CONTENTS

ABOUT THE AUTHORS

MATT AND SARAH ROGERS

THE SEVEN ARROWS
BIBLE READING METHOD

I remember my Bible reading habits as a teenager. I'd been raised in a Christian home and attended a faithful local church, yet I rarely read the Bible myself. I listened to others talk about the Bible and could have answered many questions about Bible stories, but I rarely opened its pages on my own. There are probably two reasons why.

First, I was just lazy and distracted. It's embarrassing for me to admit now, but so many other things felt more important. I had school to attend, sports to play, friends to see, and fun to experience. Buried way down on the priority list was reading, understanding, and obeying the Bible. Every once in awhile, I'd hear a sermon or go to a Christian camp and commit to trying to read the Bible more, but I rarely followed through. Maybe you're a lot like me. You know you should read the Bible, but you just never seem to get around to it. Here's the bad news: No book—certainly not this book—can give you a passion for God's Word. This is a desire that comes as a gift from God Himself. Until you are convinced of your need to know God, you'll never truly engage with the Bible, at least not in a consistent way.

The second reason I often failed to read the Bible was that I didn't know how. At times, I felt God stirring in me a passion for His Word, but I quickly grew discouraged because I didn't know how to understand the Bible and apply it to my life. It was far easier to let someone else read the Bible and tell me what it meant. While I can't give you a passion to know God, I can help you know God.

That's why I created the Seven Arrows method in the first place. I would meet people who had attended church for longer than you've been alive, yet they still struggled to read the Bible for themselves. Many had never learned a plan for reading the Bible well, and as a result, they rarely picked up their Bibles. Instead, they depended on others to tell them what the Bible said. I wanted to do something to help these people and others like them read the Bible.

I remember meeting with a young man in his late teens who had recently become a Christian. He was having a particularly hard time reading and understanding the Bible. Following his baptism, he was given a new Bible, so he set about the task of learning more about the God who had saved him. But he kept getting confused and overwhelmed, and he came to me asking for help.

Following our first conversation, I spent a couple of hours thinking about how I might teach him to read the Bible well. He didn't need a class on Bible reading, but a simple method he could use to help him ask good questions to better understand the author's meaning and apply the truth to his life. I wrote out seven questions that I ask when I read a Bible passage, then I attached a corresponding arrow to each question hoping that these arrows would be an easy way to help my friend remember these questions. That's my hope for you too.

 ARROW 1
What does this passage say?

The first step is to summarize the passage in your own words. Think about what would happen if you spent 30 minutes on the phone with your best friend. In that time, you would have talked about all sorts of things, but there are likely one or two big ideas that you focused on. Maybe you complained about today's test or maybe you talked about your plans for the weekend. If you were asked to describe the phone call later, you wouldn't describe every detail of the call. You might say, "We talked about how difficult today's Spanish test was."

You should be able to do the same thing with any passage of Scripture—simply read the passage and put the main point in your own words. You might say something like, "Jesus said that people who are really great in this world are those who serve others" or "Paul said that all people sin and disobey God."

 ARROW 2
What did this passage mean to its original audience?

Long before we can apply the Bible to our lives, we have to ask what the passage meant to those who experienced the stories of the Bible firsthand. It's easy to get bogged down on this question and think that you have to be an expert on the people and places of the Bible in order to answer it, but that's not necessarily the case. You might find it helpful to read the introduction to the book of Scripture you are reading or take a look at some study notes in your Bible, but you can often answer this question just by putting yourself in the scene and asking what you'd imagine those in the story would have thought or felt.

For example, you might read about Jesus' interaction with the woman at the well in John 4 and conclude that she would have been embarrassed by her sin, but also amazed that Jesus showed love and compassion to her anyway.

↑ ARROW 3
What does this passage tell us about God?

The Bible is about God, so it's wise to ask ourselves what we learn about Him when we read each passage. This question is important because it protects us from making ourselves the main character in the Bible. It's easy to read the Bible as if it's actually about us—our problems, our struggles, our needs. But that's not the case. The Bible is about God and His story, and it's an honor that He would include us.

There will be times when the Bible just comes right out and tells us something about God. We might read that God is gracious, compassionate, or faithful. Other times, it may not be as clear, and we have to think about the story and consider how God's character is seen. Also, sometimes Scripture will refer to God the Father, but other times we learn something about Jesus or the Holy Spirit.

↓ ARROW 4
What does this passage tell us about man?

Once you've asked the first three questions, it's time to turn the attention to your own life by asking what you learn about yourself from the passage you read. This question will likely be one of the easiest for you to answer because you know yourself well. Since the Bible is the story of God's work to save sinners like you, then you will see people who sin (like you do) and need Jesus (like you do) throughout the stories you read.

→ ARROW 5
What does this passage demand of me?

The final three arrows are action-oriented. They ask you to do something based on the truth you've discovered in arrows one through four. You will find that some passages make the application clearer than others. In many of Paul's letters, he comes right out and tells you what you should do: live a life of love, don't grumble or complain, and the list goes on and on. Other times you'll have to reflect on the passage you've read and consider the application based on your answers to the first four questions.

One word of caution: This application is not always a physical action. For example, you might find that some application will focus on your thoughts more than your actions—things like *trust God* or *don't worry*. This may not seem like an action, but these steps of obedience are just as important as other more easily observed actions.

 ARROW 6
How does this passage change the way I relate to people?

Arrow six forces a specific type of application—one that challenges you to apply the Bible to the various relationships in your life. You might think of it this way—the Bible pushes us toward two types of application, vertical and horizontal. Vertical application is primarily directed toward God—things like prayer, trust, and faith. Horizontal application is directed toward other people.

This arrow calls us to consider how the passage would have us love the people God has put in our lives. Maybe it's sharing the gospel with a friend who doesn't know Jesus. Maybe it's apologizing to someone we've hurt or serving someone in need. Combined, arrows five and six help us to obey both aspects of one of the greatest commandments as we seek to love God and love others.

 ARROW 7
What does this passage prompt me to pray to God?

The final arrow in our Bible reading process invites us to talk to God about what we've read. Prayer should be a response to God for the ways He has spoken to us through His Word. It's the same way we would interact with a friend who sent us a text. We would read what our friend said, and then reply with our own message.

Relationships require interaction and communication, and the same is true of our relationship with God. We listen to Him speak to us through His Word, and then we respond back to Him in prayer. Prayer based on the Bible allows us to ask specifically and intentionally for those things God has shown us in His Word, rather than merely praying for whatever comes to our mind in the moment.

INTRODUCTION

The Bible can be an intimidating book. Its sheer size makes it unlike most books you might pick up. Then once you start reading, it can be overwhelming. There are so many names you may not recognize, stories that seem downright strange, and concepts that are hard to make sense of. It's easy to give up before you even try to read the Bible for yourself.

Once you get past the intimidation factor, you might find that the Bible isn't nearly as complex as you think. Of course, we are reading the story of the God of the universe and His work in the world, so we can expect that story to be challenging at times. In fact, the best thinkers in all of the world will never understand everything there is to know about God. But God did something amazing in giving us the Bible. He took the truth about Himself and His work in the world and put them into words. He gave us a book that is meant to show us what He is like, how we can know Him, and what we are to do with our lives. We would be foolish to take such a gracious gift and assume we can't understand it. We can understand the Bible because God wants to be known.

It might help you to think about the Bible in a series of chapters. Every story we read has a big idea—a main point—but that concept is told in a series of chapters with many smaller stories or ideas communicated within each. The story of the Bible is about God's work, through Jesus Christ, to save sinners and a broken world from the effects of sin. A good way of organizing the story is breaking it down into nine "chapters."

- Chapter 1: Creation

- Chapter 2: Fall

- Chapter 3: Plan

- Chapter 4: People

- Chapter 5: Kingdom

- Chapter 6: Judgment

- Chapter 7: Jesus

- Chapter 8: Church

- Chapter 9: Eternity

The *Seven Arrows Devotional* is designed to move you through these chapters using the Seven Arrows method to understand the critical Bible passages in each chapter. Of course, there are more passages that could be selected, but I've attempted to provide the key sections of Scripture that will help you to understand the big story of the Bible.

You'll also notice that the last day of each week will connect that chapter of God's story to Jesus Christ, who serves as the key to understanding all of the Bible. These passages are selected to demonstrate the central role Jesus plays in uniting the Bible into a clear story of God's mission to save sinners and remake a broken world. Each day, I'll provide you with some context for the passage and will connect what you've read to the main story of the Bible. From there, you'll be ready to work through the Seven Arrows yourself.

Let's begin where every good story starts—in the beginning.

HOW TO USE

Here's how this process would work with a passage of Scripture. Let's take Psalm 19:7–11, which talks about the value of God's Word. Here's how I might use the arrows to help me understand and obey this passage. Notice that I don't try to answer each question in lengthy sentences or address every detail of the passage. What I'm trying to do is capture the main point and translate that main idea into truth I can live.

PSALM 19:7-11

7 The instruction of the LORD is perfect,

renewing one's life;

the testimony of the LORD is trustworthy,

making the inexperienced wise.

8 The precepts of the LORD are right,

making the heart glad;

the command of the LORD is radiant,

making the eyes light up.

9 The fear of the LORD is pure,

enduring forever;

the ordinances of the LORD are reliable

and altogether righteous.

10 They are more desirable than gold—

than an abundance of pure gold;

and sweeter than honey

dripping from a honeycomb.

11 In addition, your servant is warned by them,

and in keeping them there is an abundant reward.

⟲ ARROW 1 // What does the passage say?

God's Word is a treasure that is meant to explain God's truth and guide my life.

← ARROW 2 // What did the passage mean to its original audience?

The Israelites had learned many painful lessons because of their failure to obey God's Word, so they would have understood the truth of this passage.

↑ ARROW 3 // What does the passage tell us about God?

God is gracious and gives His people the gift of His Word to protect them from harm.

↓ ARROW 4 // What does the passage tell us about man?

I need to be warned and led by God's Word, because I am often tempted to disobey God and do whatever I want.

→ ARROW 5 // What does the passage demand of me?

Rather than thinking about reading the Bible as a task to complete, I should thank God for the gift of His Word and learn to treasure its wisdom.

↔ ARROW 6 // How does this passage change the way I relate to people?

I can learn to know, understand, and obey God's Word, so that I can share its truth with my friends and point them to God's plans and purposes for life.

↪ ARROW 7 // What does this passage prompt me to pray to God?

God, I thank You for Your Word. I pray that You would help me learn to love Your Word over the course of this year, so that I can know You better and love You more.

That's it. Pretty simple, right? Now, let's give you an overview of where we're going in the next 52 weeks, as we seek to use these arrows to help us understand the entire Bible.

CHAPTER 1//CREATION

The main story of creation is told in the first two chapters of the Bible. The relatively small amount of space given to the story of creation does not mean that these two chapters are insignificant. In fact, as with every story, you simply can't understand the rest of the Bible unless you understand how the story begins.

Creation introduces us to God, describing who He is and why He made everything, including men and women. We meet the first couple, Adam and Eve, who are uniquely fashioned by God for a specific purpose. This purpose continues today, and even though sin has invaded God's good world, His purpose remains the same.

These key truths, established at the beginning of the Bible, provide the foundation for your life. If there's one word that describes the season of life you're in, it would likely be "change." Everything is changing. Your physical growth is matched by changes in your experience and understanding of the world. During these years, you are coming face to face with the brokenness of the world we live in. There are so many factors in life that seem out of control and don't appear to make sense. How is anyone supposed to move through life in such an ever-changing world?

You've got three options. One, you can try to figure out life on your own. You can attempt to use your own wisdom to determine how all the pieces of your life—your gifts and abilities, your passions, your problems, your past failures—fit together and make sense. Two, you can give up on trying to make sense out of life. You can follow your passions and try to make the best out of life on your own without the slightest concern for what you were put on this earth to do.

Or, the final option is to look to God. You could recognize that your knowledge is limited and seek God's wisdom. You could ask hard questions like: Is there a God? If there is a God, how can I know Him? What did God put me on this earth to do? How can I pursue what I'm created for? These questions are difficult, and many people don't ask them. But, if you really want answers, God has already given them to you in His Word.

GENESIS 1:1-2

There was never a time when God did not exist. Our Bible begins with the story of creation, yet God existed long before He created the world. Genesis 1 begins "in the beginning" of human history but it is not the beginning of God's story. He is eternal—meaning that He always was and always will be. It's hard for us to get our minds around this reality. Our lives seem so big most days—we've got so much to do, so many people competing for our attention, and so many things that make us worry about the future. We can easily lose sight of the fact that God is so much bigger than we are. He was at work long before we were born and will continue to exist long after our lives are over. Since our lives are so small in comparison, it's critical that we understand our lives from the perspective of God's story. Who is God? Why did He create all things? The answers to these questions help us catch a glimpse of how our lives fit within the great story that the eternal God is writing in the world.

What does this passage say?

_____

_____

_____

What did this passage mean to its original audience?

_____

_____

_____

What does this passage tell us about God?

_____

_____

_____

What does this passage tell us about man?

_____

_____

_____

What does this passage demand of me?

_____

_____

_____

How does this passage change the way I relate to people?

_____

_____

_____

What does this passage prompt me to pray to God?

_____

_____

_____

DAY 2

GENESIS 1:3-19

God's words are powerful. They are not like the words you and I say every day. Our words can make someone laugh or cry; they can encourage or wound. We use words to communicate our feelings, to get a friend to do us a favor, or even to write a new song or poem. Sometimes our words have the desired effect, but they often lack power. People ignore us, they don't listen or do what we want, but God's words are very different. He created everything with His words—the sun and the moon, the mountains and the valleys, lions and bears—everything! He simply spoke and all of the things we see every day were created from nothing. That's some kind of power. But this power wasn't simply on display at creation. God continues to use His Word to show His power. Today, by His Word, God creates new life in those who were once dead in their sins. And the same power that once spoke all things into existence, speaks to you through the Bible you now hold in your hands.

↻

_____

_____

_____ ←

_____

_____

_____ ↑

_____

_____

_____ ↓

_____

_____

_____ →

_____

_____

_____ ↔

_____

_____

_____ ↰

_____

_____

GENESIS 1:26-31

↻ _____
_____
_____
← _____
_____
_____
↑ _____
_____
_____
↓ _____
_____
_____
→ _____
_____
_____
↔ _____
_____
_____
↪ _____
_____
_____

The high point of God's creation is people, like you and me. God made everything that stuns us with its beauty or magnitude—things like the Grand Canyon or a sky full of stars on a clear night. He declared all these aspects of creation to be "good." But God called people "very good," His highest praise. This means that every person who lives has tremendous worth, and further, serves a purpose in God's great plan. We may not feel very good some days. Like creation, our bodies and emotions are broken by sin, but we were not created this way. On days when we drop the ball, feel discouraged, get bad news, or struggle with feelings of loneliness, it's critical that we remember that we were created by a good God who sees us as valuable treasures. You don't need any other validation when God has already said that you have worth.

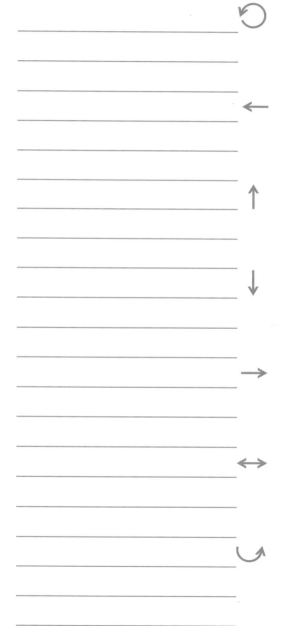

COLOSSIANS 1:15-18

When we say that God existed before creation and made all things, we are not merely speaking about God the Father. God exists in three persons—the Father, the Son, and the Holy Spirit— and each were an active part in God's creation. You may have noticed that Genesis uses plural pronouns saying, "Let us make man in our image" (Gen. 1:26a). There is one God, yet this one God exists in three persons, often referred to as the Trinity. Paul, writing in the New Testament, makes it clear that all things were created by, through, and for Jesus. We read about Jesus' birth in Matthew's Gospel, but the Son existed from the beginning and God always had a plan in place to save sinners through Jesus' work. The Holy Spirit was sent to the church in Acts 2, but the Spirit hovered over the waters of the deep from the beginning of creation. Together, the Father, Son, and Spirit created all things. Further, each continues to play a part in saving sinners and restoring the world from the effects of sin.

GENESIS 1:26-27

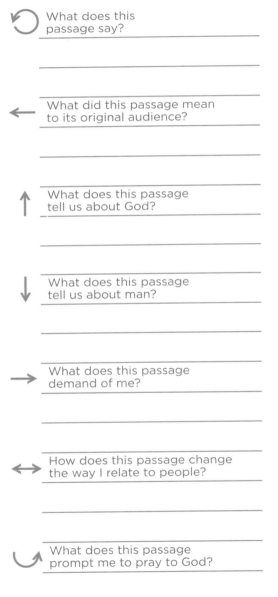

What does this passage say?

_____

_____

What did this passage mean to its original audience?

_____

_____

What does this passage tell us about God?

_____

_____

What does this passage tell us about man?

_____

_____

What does this passage demand of me?

_____

_____

How does this passage change the way I relate to people?

_____

_____

What does this passage prompt me to pray to God?

_____

_____

One concept emphasized in God's creation of men and women is that we are made "in the image of God." This certainly doesn't mean that we look like God in a physical way. There's much more to it than that. A king in the ancient Near East would often set up an image or statue in a location as a representation of His rule and character in that area. Though the king was not physically present, the people were to be reminded of him whenever they looked at the image. In a similar way, God sets up image-bearers throughout the world, so others would be reminded of His character, how He relates to people, and of the fact that God rules over creation. The only way you and I can actually fulfill that image-bearing mission is in a relationship with God through Jesus Christ.

GENESIS 1:28-31

From the beginning of creation, God gave His people a mission. He didn't simply create Adam and Eve, put them in a perfect world, and tell them to enjoy the food and take a nap. He gave them a purpose, including working. First, they were to multiply and fill the earth. This process of multiplication would allow for an increasing number of men and women who would display the image of God. Second, they were to rule over the earth. Finally, they were to enjoy God's goodness as they ate and enjoyed the good garden in which they were placed. Often, we're tempted to discount the significance of what it means to be human. Marriage, children, work, and enjoyment are all essential to the way God designed the world to function. And whereas all these were initially pure and good, today the curse of sin has caused problems and made certain aspects difficult for us. Nonetheless, they are vital and valuable ways for men and women to reflect God's image in the world.

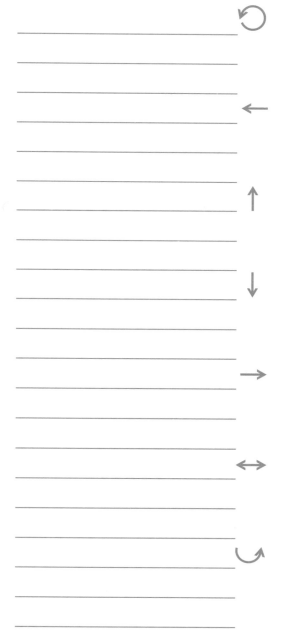

GENESIS 2:1-3

↻ _____

← _____

↑ _____

↓ _____

→ _____

↔ _____

↪ _____

Rest is the final stage in God's work of creation. But God's rest is different than our rest. We experience a long, frustrating day at school and we end up crashing on the couch as soon as we get home because our energy is depleted and we need to recharge. God is all-powerful, and He doesn't run out of energy or hit a wall like we do. Yet He rests and establishes a pattern for His people to follow. When we rest, it shows that we are dependent on God's creative power to live. Apart from God's supplying us with energy, we can't do anything. When we get tired, God graciously gives us rest and teaches us to depend on Him. That's why He established a day of rest, the Sabbath, in which people were to cease their work and rest in God's goodness and care. Today believers continue to learn to depend on God through rest, which then enables us to reflect His image well.

GENESIS 2:5-9

Genesis 2 zooms in on God's creation of men and women in a more specific way than in chapter 1. Here we see that God created Adam, the first man, in two distinct stages. First, He took dust and used it to fashion the physical body of the first man. Then, he breathed His breath into this substance and gave Adam life. The dust of the earth and the breath of God were combined to demonstrate that all people, as descendants of Adam, have a component that you can see (a physical body) and an aspect of themselves that you can't see (a soul). Both are important. With our bodies, we honor God, do meaningful work, run, jump, and play. But there's more to life than our bodies. We're also filled with the breath of God and given a unique capacity to experience His presence and interact with Him in an intimate and personal relationship.

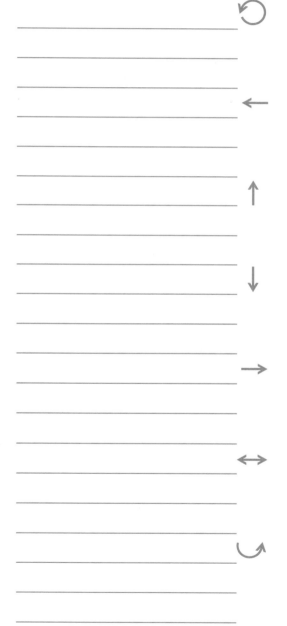

HEBREWS 1:1-3

↻ _____

_____

← _____

_____

↑ _____

_____

↓ _____

_____

→ _____

_____

↔ _____

_____

↰ _____

_____

The author of Hebrews applies the language of image-bearing to Jesus, who is described as "the exact expression of His nature." Sometimes you might hear it said that a child looks like his or her parents. The child's facial features or physical characteristics are designed in such a way that they model one parent or the other. Yet, no children are the exact imprints of their parents. In the same way, no person God makes is His perfect image. Sin makes this impossible. We all fall short of our created design, but there is one whose image reflects God perfectly all the time because He is God! Jesus is not made in the image of God; He is the image of God. If we want to know what God is like, the writer of Hebrews reminds us, we should look no further than Jesus. When we see His love for others, His compassion for the broken, His willing and humble service, His sacrificial death, and His victorious resurrection, we see a perfect picture of God.

GENESIS 2:15-17

As the story continues, the author of Genesis zooms in on God's creation of men and women in a very specific way. Men and women were given a task to work and develop the garden that served as their home. Though God made all things good, His design was that people would play a role in enhancing His good world, and God gave one clear rule that would provide a boundary for their work. They were free to enjoy all of God's good creation except the fruit of one tree which God declared to be off limits. He's the Creator of all things, so He knew that it was best for Adam and Eve to avoid this tree. As they submitted to God's plan, they had the privilege of working God's great creation and developing it to increasingly show off His greatness. The same is true today. We can invest our lives and God-given gifts in various aspects of God's world to help others see how great God is. Science, architecture, mathematics, arts, education, and sports are all ways we can invest our lives to work and develop the world in which He's placed us.

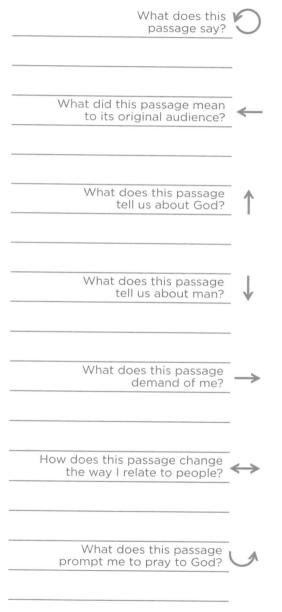

What does this passage say?

What did this passage mean to its original audience?

What does this passage tell us about God?

What does this passage tell us about man?

What does this passage demand of me?

How does this passage change the way I relate to people?

What does this passage prompt me to pray to God?

GENESIS 2:18-22

_____
_____

← _____
_____

↑ _____
_____

↓ _____
_____

→ _____
_____

↔ _____
_____

↪ _____
_____

At some point, God saw something wrong with His good creation. He said is was not good that Adam was alone, so God continued His creation work by fashioning a woman from Adam's rib. God united the man and woman in marriage and set them out together on the mission of reflecting His image throughout creation. In Genesis 1 and 2, we notice that God created two unique and specific genders—men and women. Both genders are equally made in the image of God and with equal worth that comes from their Creator. They are, however, created with different physical characteristics and different roles to play within God's creation. These differences do not make one gender more valuable than the other. Rather they reflect the magnificence of His intricate care ensuring that the world is able to fulfill His mission through the uniqueness of men and women living as His image-bearers.

GENESIS 2:24-25

Have you ever wondered where marriage came from? Here, we see marriage was part of God's design from the beginning. The uniting of a man and a woman in marriage was His plan for filling the earth with image-bearers. He intentionally designed Adam and Eve to serve as complements in this mission. Adam and Eve set the pattern of marriage for the rest of human history, as a man and a woman leaving their biological families and uniting to one another in order to partner together to fulfill God's mission. This means that the decisions we make regarding who we may date and eventually marry are full of life-shaping significance. Perhaps no decision you make influences the path of your life more than finding a godly spouse with whom you can pursue God's mission together. This process does not lie outside the realm of God's concern, nor is it merely an area where you should feel shame and guilt over poor decisions from your past. Rather, the choice of a spouse is a spiritual decision meant to be made through the pursuit of wisdom from others and a deep dependence on God's leadership. These help us make wise decisions and enable us to fulfill God's mission for our lives.

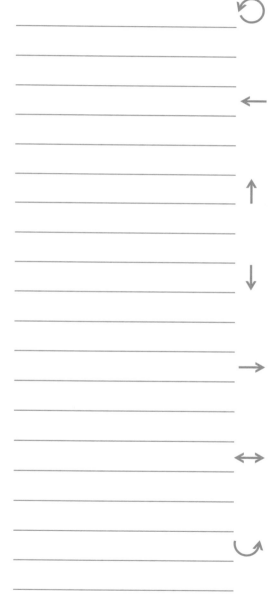

ISAIAH 43:1-7

↺ _____

← _____

↑ _____

↓ _____

→ _____

↔ _____

↩ _____

The prophet Isaiah reflected on God's creation making a very important point. He declared that God created all people for His glory. "Glory" is not likely a word you use every day, but the idea is one you experience all the time. Glory is used to describe something that is great, significant, or weighty. After a day of hiking, we might say that the mountaintop view is absolutely glorious. Glory is greatness intensified. It's an apt description for God. The combination of all of His attributes—His love, wisdom, and beauty—are so great that the word "great" will hardly do. God is glorious. Isaiah reminds us that He created men and women to declare and demonstrate this glory. How do we do this? We give Him glory when we fulfill the mission for which we were created by reflecting His image. We're meant to live the kind of lives that cause others to see and respond to the glory of our great God.

JOHN 17:1-5

John records Jesus' prayer immediately prior to His brutal crucifixion. This prayer, often known as the High Priestly Prayer, reveals to us the intimacy Jesus had with the Father, and it gives us an insider's perspective on the way in which He understood His life's mission. His prayer astounds us because, coming to the end of His life, He said that He had finished the work He was put on the earth to do. He even tells us exactly what this work was—to glorify God on earth. Like all people, Jesus' life mission was to demonstrate the greatness of God. Unlike us, however, Jesus was able to do it perfectly. Everything He did—the miracles He performed, the sermons He preached, the cross He faced, the death He defeated—shouted to the world that God is great! Jesus' life is a stunning testimony to a life well-lived.

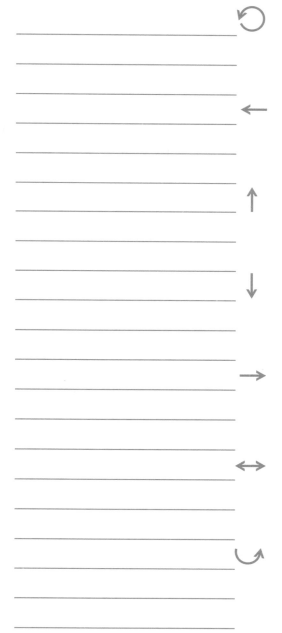

PSALM 19:1-6

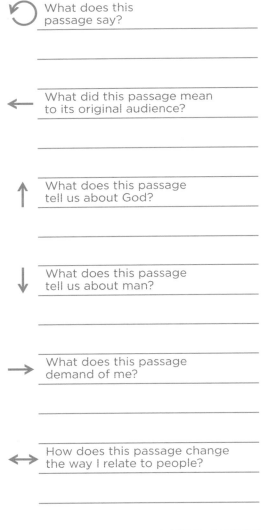

What does this passage say?

What did this passage mean to its original audience?

What does this passage tell us about God?

What does this passage tell us about man?

What does this passage demand of me?

How does this passage change the way I relate to people?

What does this passage prompt me to pray to God?

All of creation does, in a sense, what God meant specifically for people to do—proclaim the glory of the one, true God. It's not simply that God's glory can be seen in creation, but that creation speaks—it shouts—that God is great. If you've ever walked outside on a clear night and stared at the stars, you know this to be true. As you look up, you sense that there is something more to life than what you can see. There's Someone behind it all—Who made it all. You feel small and somehow captivated by the power and majesty of the Creator. It's no wonder that people have long been tempted to worship the stars, moon, and sun as gods. They are amazing! But they're amazing because they point beyond themselves to the God who spoke them into existence. If creation leaves us awestruck, imagine how great God must be.

PSALM 139:13-16

The Psalmist describes the intimate care that God took in creating men and women. The language here is personal—He intricately knitted every person together in their mothers' wombs. Every detail was fashioned by the hand of the all-powerful, ever-creative God. Like Adam and Eve before, everyone is hand-made by God. Not only that, but God also knows the length of our lives before we're ever born. Though death may be scary, we can trust that God was intentional in creating us in specific ways and for specific purposes. There will certainly be times when we're all tempted to forget this fact. There may be times when we don't like ourselves very much, times when we doubt whether God knew what He was doing when He made us like He did. Rather than growing bitter at God for the things we don't like, we should consider how every aspect of who we are is designed to help us accomplish God's mission for our lives.

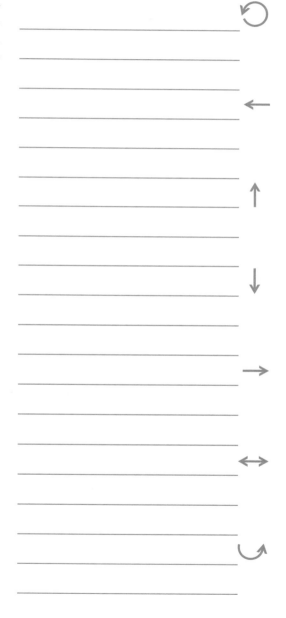

DAY 18

ACTS 17:22-34

↻ _____

_____

_____

← _____

_____

_____

↑ _____

_____

_____

↓ _____

_____

_____

→ _____

_____

_____

↔ _____

_____

_____

↪ _____

_____

_____

The speech recorded in Acts 17 took place as Paul and his band of missionaries traveled to tell people the good news of Jesus' work and establish new churches. In Athens, Paul found that the people worshiped a lot of false gods, so he took the opportunity to speak to them about the one true and living God. Paul began with creation—declaring to anyone listening that the true God is the one who made the heavens and the earth. There's no god but the Creator God. Not only that, but the true God populated the world with image-bearers—descendants of Adam and Eve. He did this very specifically. He intentionally determined the exact time and place that every person—including you—would be born. God was at work long before you were born, placing you in such a way that you could display His image and fulfill your life's purpose.

REVELATION 4:1-11

It may seem strange to include a passage from the book of Revelation in a chapter where we are learning about God's creation. But that's the beauty of the Bible. From start to finish, the Bible tells one story of God's plan for men and women to do what they were created to do—reflect His image throughout all the earth to bring Him glory. In the book of Revelation, John describes a future scene, when those who have been saved by God and remade in His image will gather around the throne in worship. It's then we will fully know and experience the glory of God in a world that is free from sin. We're told that God's creation will still be on the minds of men and women far in the future. There the world will be whole again—perfect and no longer broken by the implications of sin—and we will see clearly that God's glorious creation is very good indeed.

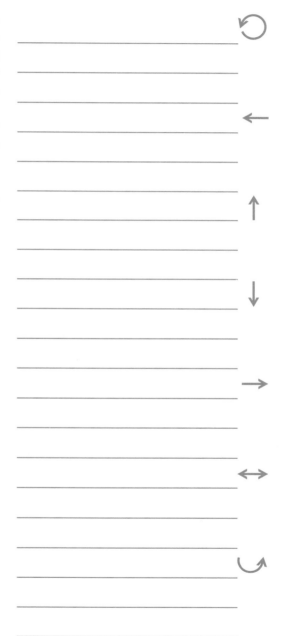

JOHN 1:1-18

↻ _____

_____

← _____

_____

↑ _____

_____

↓ _____

_____

_____

→ _____

_____

_____

↔ _____

_____

_____

↩ _____

_____

_____

John begins his Gospel a bit differently than Matthew, Mark, and Luke. He introduces Jesus as the Word of God who was at work in the beginning. Not only was the Word present at the dawn of creation, but this word was God. Centuries later, the Word of God did something amazing—He put on flesh and came to this earth as a man, Jesus Christ. This is not to say that Jesus was some sort of mythical creature who disguised himself as a person. Though His birth was unique, Jesus was fully human—and He was also fully God. He invaded a dark and broken world with the light of the glory of God, the very same God who spoke all things into being and willingly humbled Himself to come to earth knowing that He would face a brutal end because of His love for the men and women He created. God did not stand back and watch as people rebelled from His goodness; rather, He pursued wayward sinners with love by coming to them Himself. This mission was necessary because of the horrible choices Adam and Eve made in the next chapter of God's story.

CHAPTER 2//FALL

The second chapter in God's story is filled with tragedy. In fact, every bad thing you've ever experienced can be explained by this portion of God's story. It's almost unbelievable something like this, with such far reaching consequences, could happen.

Adam and Eve had all they could want and more! They had a perfect creation, filled with beauty and free from pain. They had more than enough food, and all of it was fresh and delicious. They had each other—two people God had brought together in marriage so that neither would be alone. They even had good work to do. Each day was spent developing various aspects of the world so that God's beauty, power, wisdom, and greatness could be experienced. And they had God! They walked and talked with the Creator of the Universe as you and I might relate to a friend.

In one fatal act, however, they rebelled against God and pursued what He told them to avoid. They sinned, and their sin brought life-shaping, world-changing implications—pain and suffering that we still experience today.

We live in a world that knows brokenness all too well. Everywhere we look, things are messed up. We read about God's creation and struggle to imagine such a reality because it's so different from our everyday experience. Our world is filled with people who die, marriages that end in divorce, teens who commit suicide, friendships that are broken, starving people, and on and on we could go.

If we look closely, however, we notice that the problem isn't just with other people; it's in us as well. We do all sorts of foolish, evil things. In fact, we find that we are incapable of doing what is right most days. We say things we shouldn't, think thoughts we'd like to deny, treat people in ways that hurt rather than help, act in ways that cause shame and guilt. We've got a big problem in our hearts to go along with the mess in our world.

This next chapter will describe where all of that sin came from and the effect it had on God's good creation. We will see why Adam and Eve sinned and the implications of their foolish choice on their image-bearing mission. And we'll be introduced to the ways their sin affects every person—both externally in the world and internally in our hearts. Along the way, we'll also see little glimmers of hope because God was already at work doing something about sin. But before we can get to the good news, we've got to understand some really, really bad news.

GENESIS 3:1-5

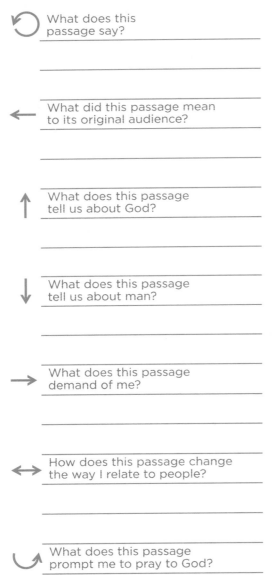

What does this
passage say?

What did this passage mean
to its original audience?

What does this passage
tell us about God?

What does this passage
tell us about man?

What does this passage
demand of me?

How does this passage change
the way I relate to people?

What does this passage
prompt me to pray to God?

Satan, in the form of a serpent, appeared on the scene in Genesis 3. His question to the woman reveals that he intended to cause the man and woman to doubt God's word and God's goodness. Clearly, Satan's first question was based on mistruth. God actually said that they could eat of *every* tree of the Garden except one. The woman's reply also contains error—God did not say that they should not *touch* the fruit of that tree, only that they were not to eat it. The serpent then undermined God's word by declaring that Adam and Eve had nothing to worry about by disobeying God. In fact, he told them that by eating the fruit, they would become like God, knowing good and evil. But this was not God's design. He created image-bearers to depend on Him. He set the standard for what was good and evil, expecting them to live by faith—to listen to His Word, trust Him, and obey. Sadly, they didn't. And neither do we.

GENESIS 3:6-7

The Bible gives three reasons the woman listened to Satan and ate the fruit of the one forbidden tree: (1) The fruit was good for food, (2) it was a delight to the eyes, and (3) it was desirable for wisdom. She trusted in her own assessment of the situation rather than trusting God's word. Adam, who was right there with her, followed her lead and ate of the fruit. Immediately, the first couple knew something was wrong and tried to cover up the implications of their sin. We all make the same mistake. Sin promises something we desire, and, rather than obeying God and refusing sin, we trust our own desires to guide our actions. But sin always over-promises and under-delivers, and once we've sinned, we recognize that we've messed up. We'd all be far better off if we would simply hear God's Word, trust His wisdom, and do what He says.

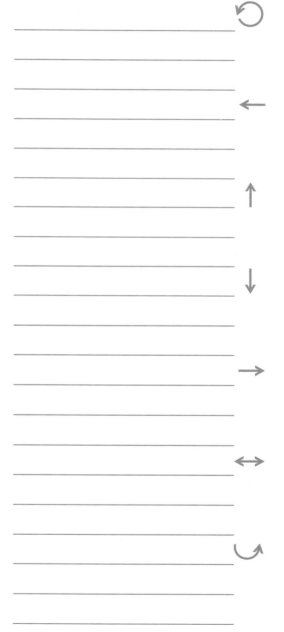

GENESIS 3:8-13

The story told in these verses is almost comical. The Creator of the Universe was walking in the garden He made by simply speaking it into existence. Adam and Eve—who God fashioned using His very hands—were there in the garden after eating from the tree God had told them to avoid. Their responses are a picture of how we all respond when we sin. First, they tried to hide from God. Can you imagine Adam trying to duck down behind a bush in hopes that God wouldn't see him? Then, they started pointing fingers in blame. The man blamed the woman and pointed out that it was God who gave him this foolish woman in the first place. The woman likewise pointed to the serpent and blamed his deceit for her choice. They were busted in their sin and they knew it, but they were unwilling to take the blame for their sin and ask for forgiveness. Each of us is also prone to run from God when we sin even though He sees and knows everything we have ever done or will ever do.

GENESIS 3:14-19

The consequences for sin were immediate. Because God is holy, He could not look the other way and pretend that Adam and Eve had not disobeyed Him. His punishments began with the serpent—whose life would now be spent crawling on its stomach and would one day suffer death at the hands of Eve's offspring. Way back in Genesis, God revealed a plan to destroy Satan. Though, at this point in the story, no one knew who this offspring would be. The story of the Old Testament traces the child of Eve through generations all the way to Jesus, the fulfillment of this promise. The judgment did not stop with Satan, however. Both the woman and the man suffered as well. Childbirth would be painful, work would be difficult, and relationships would become strained. And perhaps worst of all, Adam and Eve would suffer death as a penalty for their sin. Rather than live forever subject to the curse of sin, they would return to the dust from which they were made.

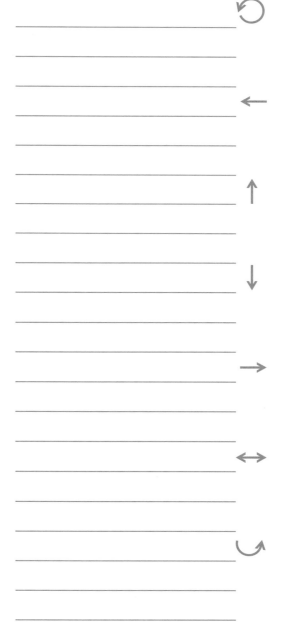

ROMANS 5:12-21

Paul's letter to the church in Rome was filled with complexity. In many ways, it's a summary of everything Paul wrote in his other letters. In writing the letter, Paul began with creation and explained God's story from start to finish. So, you'd expect it to be a bit hard to understand in places. We will return to this letter often. Notice in today's passage that Paul compared two men: Adam and Jesus. Adam, as the first man, stands as the head of the entire human race. Paul said that his sinful choice in the Garden did not merely affect Adam and Eve. Rather, Adam's sin was passed down to every generation that followed, and we are all now born in trespasses and sins. This is why we all live in ways we know are wrong. Sin lies at the core of who we are, making it impossible for us to fulfill our image-bearing mission. Paul contrasts Adam's failure with Jesus, the promised seed of the woman, who stands as the head of a new humanity. His perfect life, unlike Adam's miserable choice, can be given to those who trust Him by faith.

GENESIS 3:20-21

These two verses are some of the most beautiful in all of the Bible. They come on the heels of the tragic choice of Adam and Eve to rebel against God's commands, and this passage gives us a picture of God's love and grace. First, humanity continues to live. God had every right to kill Adam and Eve on the spot, but he didn't—He lavished grace upon them. Further, He allowed Eve to have children, making her the mother of all the living. From these children would one day come the promised child who would crush the head of Satan forever. Second, God clothed Adam and Eve. Remember, back in Genesis 3:7, Adam and Eve tried to cover themselves after they'd sinned. But they could not cover their sin— only God can do that. So He killed an animal and used its skin to cover their nakedness. Here is the first mention of a theme that will be common throughout the Old Testament—the living must die in order to cover the sins of the men and women who deserve death.

What does this passage say?

_____

_____

_____

What did this passage mean to its original audience?

_____

_____

What does this passage tell us about God?

_____

_____

What does this passage tell us about man?

_____

_____

What does this passage demand of me?

_____

_____

How does this passage change the way I relate to people?

_____

_____

What does this passage prompt me to pray to God?

_____

_____

_____

GENESIS 3:22-24

↺ _____

_____

_____

← _____

_____

_____

↑ _____

_____

↓ _____

_____

_____

→ _____

_____

_____

↔ _____

_____

_____

↱ _____

_____

_____

God's holiness and man's sinfulness cannot coexist because holiness destroys sin. God didn't want to destroy people who had become sinful, so He threw Adam and Eve out of the garden and gave them over to their own choices. By their sinful actions, they said, in effect, that they would prefer to live out from under God's rule and reign. They wanted to do their own thing—to make their own decisions about right and wrong. But God's rules are not arbitrary, and He knew all along what was best for Adam and Eve. He knew what they'd lose as a result of sin, and now, Adam and Eve would also know. They were sent out from the presence of the Lord, never to return to the pristine garden. From this flows the central question that only the Bible answers—How will sinful humanity ever experience relationship with God and live in His presence again?

EPHESIANS 2:1-3

Writing to the church in a city called Ephesus, Paul summarized the good news of Jesus. Before he got to the good news, Paul pointed out the depth of human sin and told the church that all people—regardless of their gender, age, ethnicity, financial status, or religious background—are born dead in sin. From birth, this is every person's position. We aren't sick and in need of a little medicine to make ourselves better—rather, we are dead and totally incapable of pleasing God. Therefore, we are destined to be permanently separated from God's presence. This is expressed in people's following the lies of Satan and the sinful patterns of the world. As a result of this sin, we all deserve the wrath of God—His rightful judgment for our sin. This bad news sets the stage for the life that can be found through faith in Jesus' work.

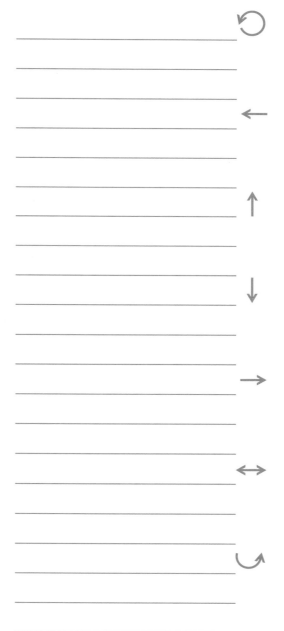

DAY 29

ROMANS 8:18-23

↺ _____
_____
← _____
_____
_____
↑ _____
_____
↓ _____
_____
_____
→ _____
_____
_____
↔ _____
_____
↰ _____
_____
_____

Sin's effects are far reaching. Creation itself is broken, and we can see this plainly in natural disasters, such as earthquakes, tornadoes, and hurricanes, among other things. Paul described these acts as earth's experiencing the pain of childbirth. Right now, the world groans, but soon new life will come. One day, this broken earth will be made right again. Our bodies are also broken. People are still made in God's image and given the mission of reflecting Him in the world, but now our bodies suffer through sickness, disease, and aging. These physical signs of brokenness are a testimony to the fact that we are dead in sin. Like the world, we, too, long for the day when our bodies will be made new—the time when no one we love will die of cancer, when we won't have to take medicine, and when we'll never get sick or injured. For now, we live in a world that sin has broken. However, because of Jesus there is hope for the future.

ROMANS 3:21-25

Paul connects a number of different parts of God's story in this short section of Romans 3. God gave the Israelites the law (we will talk about this in the next chapter) to show them God's standard for holiness and how they fall desperately short. But it is not the law that makes them fall short. All people—those who have the law and those who don't—sin and fall short of God's glory. They aren't great like God. They aren't holy like God. They don't love like God. Simply put—sinful humans don't do a great job reflecting God's image. Jesus changes all this. He offered His life to take the wrath of God for sin and bring His people back into right relationship with God. This allows God to be just—Jesus received our judgment—and also to be a justifier, because He saves sinful men and women through their faith in Jesus' work. If you find this a bit confusing, hang on tight. We'll return to this concept again and again over the coming weeks. For now, just remember that all people are born sinners, and therefore can't reflect God properly. However, Jesus changes all this through His death and resurrection.

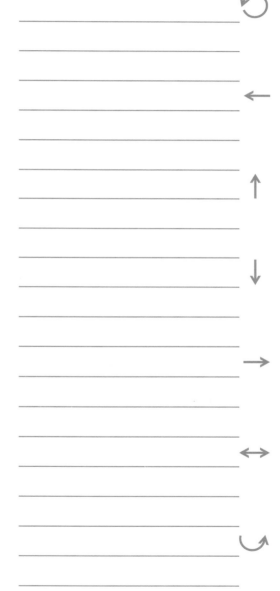

ROMANS 1:18-23

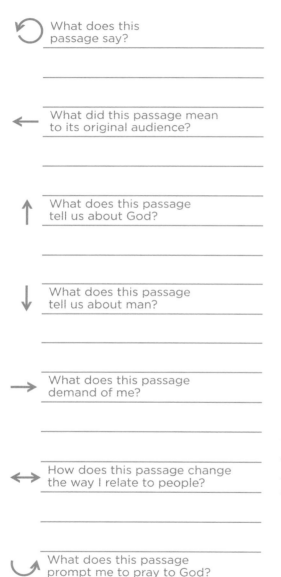

What does this passage say?

_____

_____

What did this passage mean to its original audience?

_____

_____

What does this passage tell us about God?

_____

_____

What does this passage tell us about man?

_____

_____

What does this passage demand of me?

_____

_____

How does this passage change the way I relate to people?

_____

_____

What does this passage prompt me to pray to God?

_____

_____

_____

We've already read a description of Adam and Eve's sin, the consequences they received from God, and the way their sin still affects us today. For us to truly understand the fall, however, it's important we also consider the exact nature of sin—so we know it when we see it in our lives and appreciate just what it is that Jesus delivers us from. Paul described sin in Romans using the picture of an exchange. We know this concept well. Every day we make exchanges, particularly when we spend money. We exchange a certain amount of money for food, clothes, or movie tickets. Paul said that sin is, by definition, giving glory that rightly belongs to God to some other created thing. That's a really bad switch. Rather than finding joy in celebrating God's glory, men and women love, serve, and celebrate created things as if they were God—things like popularity, money, good grades, sports, relationships, or any other thing that God has made. Anytime we value something over God, that's sin.

MATTHEW 12:33-35

The terrible exchange we read about in our last devotion comes from one place—our hearts. We love things other than God more than we love God because our hearts are twisted and broken. Our hearts don't appreciate the glory of God, instead thinking that far lesser things are more important. Jesus made this point in Matthew's Gospel, when He taught that the sinful words we speak come out of our broken hearts. He compared the process to a tree. If the tree is healthy and pure, then it will produce good fruit. If it is dead or dying, then it will produce rotten fruit, or it will not produce fruit at all. We see the fruit, but the biggest problem isn't with the fruit; it's with the source that produces the fruit. The same is true for our hearts. Our problem is not primarily that we do sinful actions, but that we have sinful hearts that consistently cause us to produce sinful thoughts, actions, and words. For true and lasting change to result we need our hearts to change, which is just what Jesus came to do.

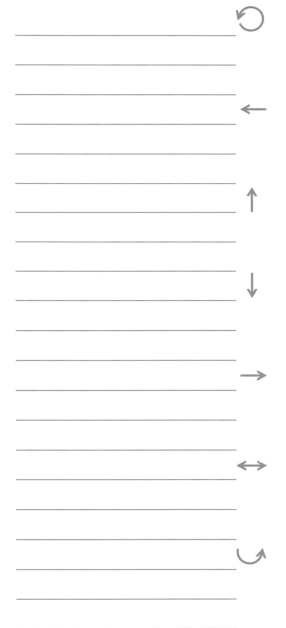

ROMANS 1:24-32

○ _____

_____

← _____

_____

_____

↑ _____

_____

↓ _____

_____

_____

→ _____

_____

_____

↔ _____

_____

_____

↰ _____

_____

_____

God defines sin as loving anything more than Him. God's purpose for each of our lives is that we would reflect Him and show how great He is. Yet sin makes it impossible for us to do that. Paul told us God's response to our foolish exchange. We've already seen that our sin means we stand condemned, and the punishment is God's wrath for eternity. But that's not all—He also allows us to feel the consequences of our sin in this life. Paul said that God gives sinners over to their desires. People choose to love other things, and God allows them to run away from Him and, much like Adam and Eve, suffer the consequences of their choices. You've likely experienced this reality in your own life. You decide to make a sinful choice. At first, it feels good so you continue to do it. But, in time, something happens. You get trapped in your sin and you begin to feel the pain. You might get busted by your parents or you may simply have to deal with the guilt of the choices you've made. Sin doesn't feel so good after a while. God gives us over so we will see that His ways are best and we should trust Him.

JAMES 1:12-15

God is not to blame for our sin. Think back to the story of Adam and Eve. He did nothing but good for them. He gave them a multitude of blessings. Even His rule about the tree was a good gift—He was protecting them from harm. Once they'd sinned, Adam and Eve could not blame God, so they pointed fingers at the serpent and one another. James, Jesus' half-brother, made the same point about the sin of all people. We can't accuse God of tempting us to sin. The problem, as we have seen, is in our own hearts. The desire to sin comes from within us, and once sin is birthed, it grows to bring death—both in this life and in the life to come. When we experience the consequences of our sin, we should never blame God, but turn to Him in repentance.

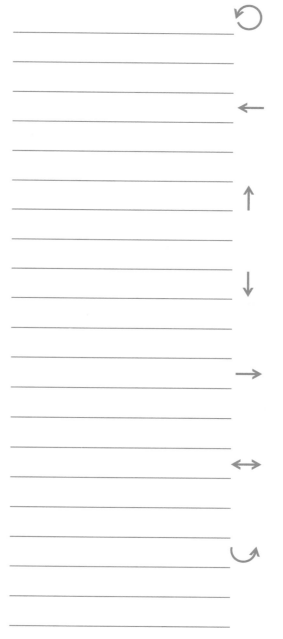

ROMANS 6:15-23

↺ _____

_____

← _____

_____

↑ _____

_____

↓ _____

_____

_____

→ _____

_____

↔ _____

_____

↰ _____

_____

_____

Paul used another image to describe sin. Sin is like slavery because it traps us in such a way that we can't stop sinning, even if we want to. Like slaves to a slave master, we are in bondage to sin. No matter how hard we try to stop, we do what our sinful hearts cause us to do. To stop sinning, we must be set free from slavery to sin, and only Jesus' work does that. Those who have faith in Him can be set free from the slave master of sin. Freed men and women do not emerge from slavery to sin and live for themselves. Instead, they become slaves to a new master—God Himself. He becomes their ruler and they are bound to do what pleases Him. All people are either slaves to sin or slaves to God—there are no other options.

CHAPTER 3//PLAN

The news in the last chapter of God's story was bad—really, really bad. But God is all powerful, and creation took simply His speaking it into existence. Therefore, couldn't God just reverse the work He'd done in creation and destroy everything He had made? Because His image-bearers introduced sin into the world and broke all of the good things He had created, He would be justified in doing so. No one could blame God for wiping out the world.

Your Bible is bigger than three pages, so you already know this is not how the story goes. God's story continues long after Genesis 3. Each page, each person, each story that follows is a compelling demonstration of God's grace and kindness. Rather than destroying everything He had made, God pursued fallen image-bearers with His love and set about the long-suffering mission of remaking the world.

We've also seen hints of the pattern by which God will make all things right. He's told us that a child of Eve will come to destroy Satan and the death that results from his work in the world. We've also seen a pattern by which God will work to address human sin—He will provide a covering for sin through the blood sacrifice of another. At this point in the story, we're not exactly sure how this will play out or how the child and the covering for sin will combine in the work of Jesus. But the plan and pattern are already in place.

The third chapter in God's story, told most clearly in the first five books of the Bible, describes the development of this plan and pattern. Throughout this chapter, we will meet many new people who will experience the craziness of life in a sin-drenched world. Some of what God does in this chapter might seem strange to us today, but try to keep your focus on the main question we're seeking to answer: How will God save sinners and fix His broken world? To answer this question, we will trace the children of Eve to determine who this savior will one day be. The answer will develop the pattern of blood sacrifice creating in us a deep appreciation for how serious God is about sin and what He's doing to make it possible for sinners to be in relationship with Him once more.

GENESIS 4:1-16

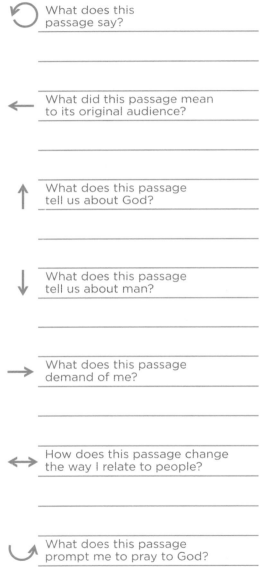

What does this
passage say?

_____

_____

← What did this passage mean
to its original audience?

_____

_____

↑ What does this passage
tell us about God?

_____

_____

↓ What does this passage
tell us about man?

_____

_____

→ What does this passage
demand of me?

_____

_____

↔ How does this passage change
the way I relate to people?

_____

_____

↪ What does this passage
prompt me to pray to God?

_____

_____

When Adam and Eve were banished from the garden, sin spread immediately. They had children and were fulfilling their mission of filling the earth. However, rather than filling the earth with people who reflect God perfectly, they were instead filling the earth with sinners. Cain killed Abel in a fit of jealousy over the way God received Abel's offering. Though Cain's final, sinful action was murder, his root sin was a heart filled with anger. And like his parents, Cain tried to cover his sin to lessen its impact. No matter how hard Cain tried to hide, God saw it all, including Cain's heart—and God judged. The sins of the first man and woman were repeated in their kids, though the nature of the sinful actions was different. It's tragic to see what happens when sin enters God's story. All the way down to the present day, we live in a world that gives overwhelming evidence of sin's effects and consequences.

GENESIS 6:1-8

There's a lot in this passage that is hard to understand. It's unclear who the people in the story are and what they are doing. What is clear is that the actions are outside of God's intentions for His world. He has allowed His people to run after the sinful things their hearts love, and the results are stunning. The author of Genesis notes the extent of sin—people are always sinning; their hearts are continually set on sin. Remember back in Genesis 1 when the author gave us insight into God's assessment of creation? He said His world was good, even very good. Only six chapters later, God grieves over His world and is saddened that He made it in the first place. But there's always hope in God's story. This passage ends by introducing Noah, a man who found favor with God and from whom God will continue His mission to save sinners and remake His world.

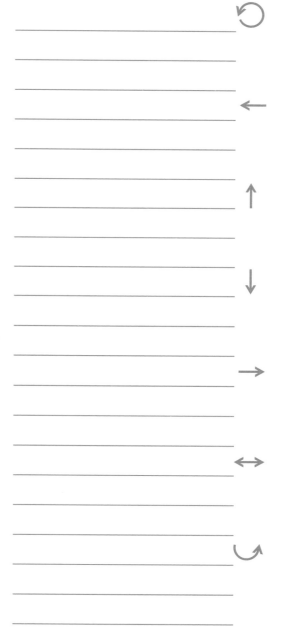

DAY 38

GENESIS 6:9-22

↺ _____
_____
_____

← _____
_____
_____

↑ _____
_____
_____

↓ _____
_____
_____

→ _____
_____
_____

↔ _____
_____
_____

↳ _____
_____
_____

God worked through Noah to preserve His image-bearers and the world He made. God told Noah that He planned to destroy the earth and its inhabitants with a flood. He warned Noah of the impending judgment and told him that He would protect Noah and his family in a most unlikely way. He instructed Noah to build an ark on which his family and two of every living creature would live while the earth was flooded. But there was a problem—Noah had never seen a flood, and he had certainly never built a boat the size God was telling him to build. But he acted in faith, based on God's word, and built the boat anyway. Noah's faith was a perfect picture of what God desires for His people today. By faith, sinners can be saved from the coming wrath of God by trusting in the way He established to save men and women.

GENESIS 8:13–9:7

God always stays faithful to His promises. He promised Noah protection from the judgment brought upon the world because of sin. Though the process of salvation was unlike anything Noah had ever experienced, he trusted God's promises and God rewarded his obedience. You can imagine the relief that accompanied Noah and his family as they stepped off the ark for the first time. They looked around at a world vastly different from the one they'd known prior to climbing on board the ark. Though much had changed, they received God's grace and favor in a remarkable way. Then God spoke, and His words were very similar to His original instructions to Adam and Eve. Once again, God described humans as made in His image, even though they were at this point broken by sin. He gave them the task of multiplying and filling the earth. Just in case there's any confusion, God reiterates that His mission has not changed, even though it would now take a powerful act of God to make it possible for sinful humans to fulfill His plan.

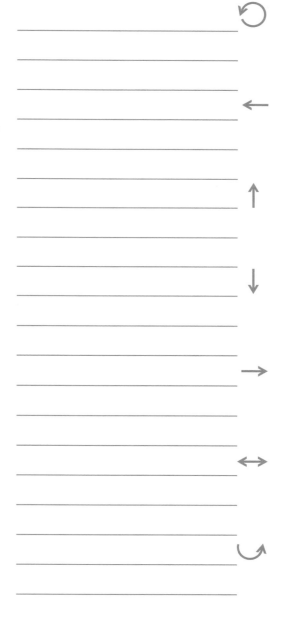

ROMANS 5:6-11

↻ _____

_____

_____

← _____

_____

_____

↑ _____

_____

↓ _____

_____

_____

→ _____

_____

_____

↔ _____

_____

↪ _____

_____

_____

God used the ark to save Noah from His wrath. God rightly judged the world for its sin, but He also graciously provided a way for people to be saved from His wrath. This is what God does. Because of His character, He must judge sin—and He does. He doesn't have to provide a way of escape, yet He does. Jesus is God's way of escape for sinners. Paul explained that God did not wait for us to get our act together or earn His love. We were dead, and much like the people of Noah's day, should face the death that our sin demands. But God sent Jesus to pay the price our sin deserves, so that we can have faith in Him and be saved from the wrath of God. The salvation offered through Jesus is much more significant than what Noah found in the ark. Though his life was spared from the flood, Noah's death was only delayed. The ark was not a permanent solution from God's wrath. Faith in Jesus will not spare us from physical death, but it does provide lasting hope that we will be saved forever from the wrath of God.

GENESIS 11:1-9

Genesis 11 is a repeat performance of Genesis 6 in many ways. Both follow on the heels of God's creation work—one the original creation in the garden and the other God's new creation following the flood. And in each case, the people rebelled against God and His purposes in the world. At this point, humans have spread out over the face of the earth taking with them their sinful passions. At Babel, they selfishly decided to build a tower to the heavens. Rather than multiplying and filling the earth with God's image, the people settled down, gathered together, and tried to exalt themselves. They didn't succeed. In spite of their best efforts, the Almighty God had to stoop down out of heaven to see their little tower. Once again, God judged the people for their sin, this time by confusing their languages and making it impossible for them to build the tower effectively. He then accomplished in judgment what the people should have done on mission—he scattered these broken image-bearers throughout the earth. One day, because of Jesus' work, God will regather His people from the ends of the earth to reflect Him perfectly and permanently once again.

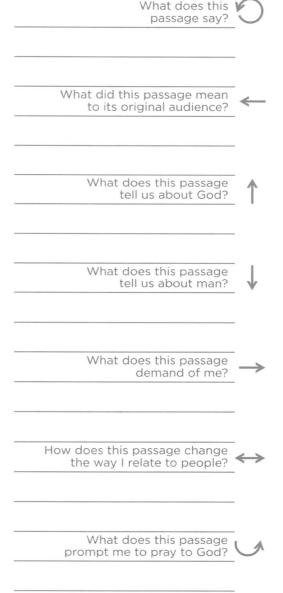

What does this passage say?

What did this passage mean to its original audience?

What does this passage tell us about God?

What does this passage tell us about man?

What does this passage demand of me?

How does this passage change the way I relate to people?

What does this passage prompt me to pray to God?

GENESIS 12:1-3

○ _____

_____

← _____

_____

↑ _____

_____

↓ _____

_____

→ _____

_____

↔ _____

_____

↺ _____

_____

There are few verses in the entire Old Testament that have as much significance as the beginning of Genesis 12. Things went from bad to worse in God's creation, yet once again God acted in His grace. He called a man named Abram and made a startling promise to him. Like Noah before, Abram was asked to respond in faith and go to an unknown country. There God promised to make His family a great nation who would serve as a blessing to all the earth. Abram's descendants were chosen as an act of God's grace to fulfill the mission He had originally given to Adam and Eve. At this point in the story, we do not know whether these people would obey faithfully, but we do know one thing—God has made a promise and He never breaks His promises. He would create a nation out of Abram's descendants, out of which all the nations of the earth would be blessed.

GENESIS 15

God made a big promise to Abram—He would have children who would flourish into a great nation, so great in fact that they would be as numerous as the stars in the heavens. Remember back in Genesis 3 when God promised Eve that she would have a child who would crush the head of the serpent? Well here we are again with the promise of a child. God had been faithful to preserve His people and the promised offspring through the flood, but it seems that the promise was threatened again because Abram was childless. It's hard to imagine having children as numerous as the stars when you don't even have a single child. But Abram did the unimaginable. He believed! He trusted in God even though God's promises didn't make sense. God even confirmed His promise in an ancient ceremony. Two people who were making a serious promise would kill animals and divide their bodies in half to create a path. The pledge makers would then walk down the path and commit to keeping their end of the promise. If they went back on their word, their end would be like the dead animals. The unique thing about God's promise is that He's the only one who walks down the path. He committed to keeping His promise to Abram regardless of what would happen in the future.

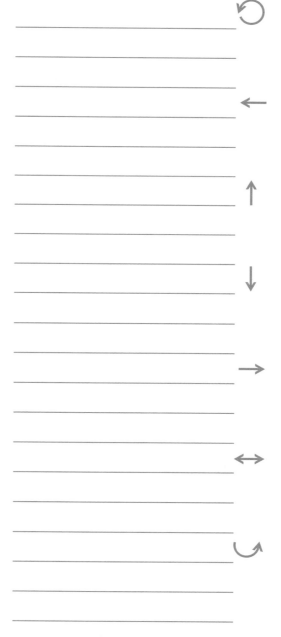

GENESIS 17

↺ _____
_____
_____
← _____
_____
_____
↑ _____
_____
_____
↓ _____
_____
_____
→ _____
_____
_____
↔ _____
_____
_____
� _____
_____
_____

The main ideas of Genesis 17 have already been mentioned in previous days. Here, however, God made it explicit that His covenant, or promise, with Abram was an everlasting one. God even changed Abram's name to Abraham to emphasize that he would be the father of many children and marked Abraham's male descendants with the sign of circumcision. God also mentioned a topic that would become common in the next books of the Bible. He said He would give Abraham's descendants land on which to live—land commonly known as the promised land. In spite of these wonderful promises, Abram still didn't have a child and was an old man by this point. Yet God promised them a child and God always keeps His promises. Soon a child would be born to this elderly couple who would continue God's faithful fulfillment of His promises to rid the world of sin.

ROMANS 4

This chapter is a mouthful. At the heart of Paul's writing is the idea of justification—or how a sinful person can be made right with God. This issue is at the core of the Bible. Paul used Abraham's life to make a comparison between two different ways a person can be made right with God. The first option would be through good works. Maybe if people are good enough, do what God says, and keep His rules, then they can earn their way back to God. The second option is through faith. They could recognize that they are sinful and incapable of being good and trust in God's promise and plan for making them right with Him once more. Paul said that Abraham's life was a picture of faith. He was not made right with God because he left his country, because he kept God's commands, or because he and his family were circumcised. In fact, each of these actions came after God's promises! His actions were simply a response to the grace of God that he'd already found, not a way to make himself right with God in the first place. Abraham had faith in God's word and this faith, not his works, made Him right with God.

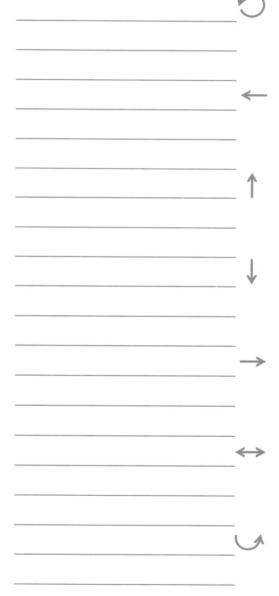

GENESIS 22:1-19

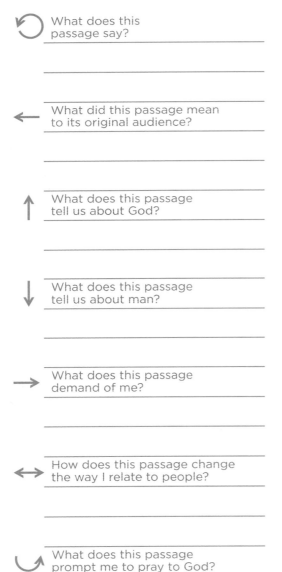

What does this passage say?

_____

_____

What did this passage mean to its original audience?

_____

_____

What does this passage tell us about God?

_____

_____

What does this passage tell us about man?

_____

_____

What does this passage demand of me?

_____

_____

How does this passage change the way I relate to people?

_____

_____

What does this passage prompt me to pray to God?

_____

_____

After years of waiting, God finally gave Abraham a child. Isaac was the firstborn son to the elderly couple and the fulfillment of God's promises. Soon after, God told Abraham to do the unthinkable—sacrifice his only son. The promised child was to die. Abraham, a man of great faith, obeyed God, even though he certainly did not understand God's reasoning. They traveled up the mountain, prepared the altar for sacrifice, and positioned Isaac on the altar to be killed. At the last minute, God provided a ram to take Isaac's place on the altar and be killed instead. Once again, God provided a sacrificial substitute for those who trusted Him in faith. We've seen this pattern repeated in the early chapters of the Bible—Noah trusted God and built an ark though he'd never seen a flood. Abram trusted God and left his country to go to an unknown land, and he demonstrated willingness to offer his only son as a sacrifice though God had promised him a large family. God's plans do not always make sense, but those who act in faith see God keep His promises in miraculous ways.

GENESIS 25:19-34

The book of Genesis tells the story of four key fathers of the Christian faith— Abraham, Isaac, Jacob, and Joseph. The lives of these four men were filled with sin, failure, romance, tragedy, success, love, and worship. At times, their actions were a demonstration of faith in God. Often they acted in ways that modeled the rebellion of their first parents, Adam and Eve. Yet through it all, God was faithful. God was intent on caring for the children through whom His promise would be fulfilled. He established a plan to ensure that future generations were protected and provided for, particularly the first-born sons in the coming generations. The first-born son would receive a birthright from his parents that would guarantee that his needs were met. Isaac's firstborn, Esau, made a regrettable exchange. He was hungry after a day in the field and decided to sell his birthright to his younger brother in exchange for some stew. Rather than resting in God's care for him, Esau attempted to get what he wanted in his own power and sold something of eternal worth for something that would only provide momentary fulfillment. This exchange is a picture of the exchange humans make when we swap God's eternal glory for the worship of things that will only bring temporary fulfillment.

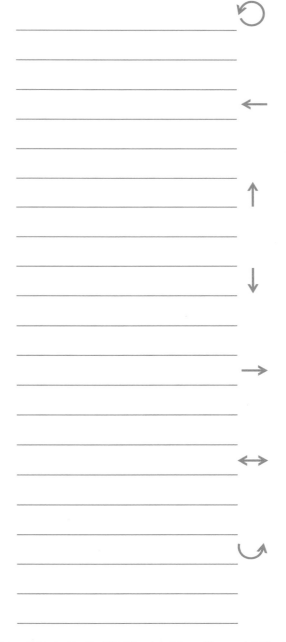

GENESIS 39

God changed Jacob's name to Israel— the name by which God's people would be known in the Old Testament—and continued to be faithful to the promises He made to Abram by blessing Israel with twelve sons, who would become the heads of the twelve tribes of Israel. The youngest son, Joseph, was the focus of attention through the later chapters of the book of Genesis. God worked through him to continue the line through which He would establish His people and send the serpent crusher. Joseph's life was far from perfect. He was sold into slavery and falsely imprisoned in Egypt. In spite of this pain, the chapter concludes by showing that God was with Joseph and was using everything in his life— even these painful experiences—to position him to accomplish God's purposes. We, too, can trust in the fact that life in a fallen world will be broken and painful, but God is at work to orchestrate every detail of our lives in order to fulfill His good purposes in and through us.

GENESIS 50:15-26

Through a unique and unexpected series of circumstances, God elevated Joseph to a key position of power in the nation of Israel. God had warned Joseph that He would strike the land with a famine, and Joseph led the nation to store up provision for the years of scarcity. More importantly, God used Joseph's position to provide for the family that once disowned him. Jacob's sons and Joseph's brothers came to Egypt for food and ended up confronting their brother face-to-face. Joseph was, at this point, in the position of power, yet he chose not to take revenge. Instead, he blessed the brothers who sold him into slavery. He concluded that even those things that seemed meant for evil could be used by God to accomplish His mission in the world. This is the story of the book of Genesis. God began by making a promise and enacted a plan in Genesis 3. Try as we might, no amount of human sin can thwart God's purposes. The book ends with the line of Eve's children still intact and another promise from God that the child will come through the tribe of Judah. God is faithful and we can trust Him.

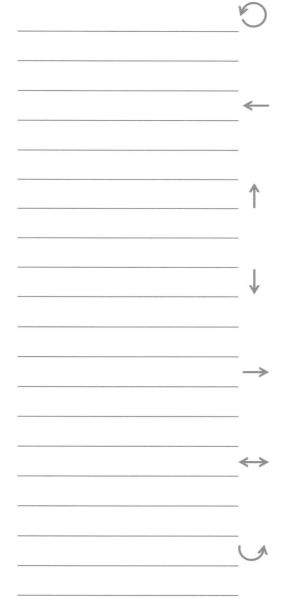

ROMANS 8:28-30

↺ _____

_____

_____

← _____

_____

_____

↑ _____

_____

_____

↓ _____

_____

_____

_____

→ _____

_____

_____

_____

↔ _____

_____

_____

↪ _____

_____

_____

In many ways, Romans 8 is the climax of the Bible. Paul described the glorious reality of Jesus' work in hope of encouraging believers living in a broken world. He reminded us that nothing we experience is permanent. There is life beyond what we can see. Like we've seen in Joseph's story, God works all things together for our good and His glory. This doesn't mean that we will understand everything that God is doing, and it certainly doesn't mean that we will like the pain we experience. But it does mean that we can find hope in the fact that God is working in ways we cannot see, and He uses our brokenness and the pain of our world for His good purposes. Central to God's purpose is the hope that we will one day be conformed to the image of Jesus. This was His mission at creation. He wanted to fill the earth with image-bearing worshipers. Sin fractured the ability of men and women to do this, yet God did not abandon His mission. He is still relentless and zealous to ensure that all those who have faith in Jesus Christ will be conformed to His image in this life and transformed into a perfect reflection of God's image in the life to come.

EXODUS 2:23-25

The beginning of the book of Exodus isn't what you might expect at this point in God's story. God's promises were being fulfilled through the nation of Israel—He was gathering a people who would reflect Him throughout the world, but they had become slaves in Egypt. After Joseph's death, the nation was enslaved to the Egyptian Pharaoh who opposed God's people. Israel grew numerically, fulfilling God's promise that they would be as many as the stars of the sky, but they weren't filling the earth as image-bearing reflections of God's glory. Yes, they were slaves in a foreign land, but God had not abandoned His people. They cried out to God, who never turned His back on them. He heard their cry, understood their pain, and remembered what He committed to do on their behalf. God then began the work of delivering His people from slavery in Egypt through his appointed leader, Moses. God does the same for His children today. When we cry out to him because of our sin, we can trust that He hears, understands, and acts on our behalf to provide a way of deliverance.

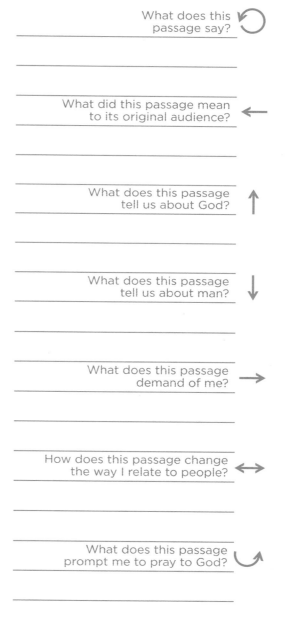

What does this passage say?

What did this passage mean to its original audience?

What does this passage tell us about God?

What does this passage tell us about man?

What does this passage demand of me?

How does this passage change the way I relate to people?

What does this passage prompt me to pray to God?

EXODUS 3

Moses was a reluctant leader. God called him to bring His people out of slavery in Egypt and lead them to the promised land. God even appeared to Moses in a miraculous way confirming that He would use Moses to deliver His people. But Moses was unsure. First, he questioned whether he was worthy of this appointment. Later in Exodus 4, he told God that the people would not listen to him and that he was not a good speaker in the first place. Even though God fashioned Moses' mouth and called him to this task, Moses questioned whether or not God could fulfill these promises through a frail leader. One final objection is important to note. Moses told God that the people would ask him who told him to come and lead them to freedom. He knew that the people would want to know if God was behind all of this or if Moses had just lost his mind. God gave Moses His name in a somewhat cryptic way. He is I Am. He is the God who is undefinable. He has always been. He is. And He will always be. He's the one, true God and people can always trust Him.

EXODUS 6:1-13

God reiterated His promises through Abraham, Isaac, and Jacob, and then through the life and work of Moses. He reminded Moses that He made a covenant with the generations before—a covenant that included them living on a land that He would give them as an act of grace. The nation of Israel was certainly not experiencing this blessing while in Egypt. They were slaves, and they were hopeless and helpless to escape. Once again, God acted. He provided deliverance for His people as a sheer act of grace, not because they deserved to find freedom. Their deliverance would come as a result of God's power. God, through Moses, would provide a miraculous escape for the people, such that no one would be tempted to think that they got themselves, by human muscle, out of slavery. If they were going to be free, it would only be because God acted on their behalf to fulfill His promises. In the same way, if anyone is forgiven from sin and escapes the wrath of God due that sin, it will only be because of God's might and power at work on their behalf.

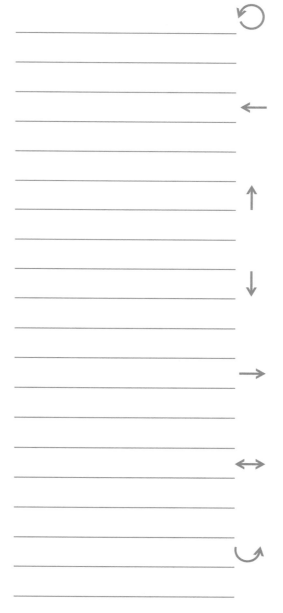

EXODUS 12

○ _____

_____

← _____

_____

↑ _____

_____

↓ _____

_____

→ _____

_____

↔ _____

_____

↪ _____

_____

God brought a series of plagues exhibiting to Pharaoh the power of God working to free His people and forcing the release of His people to the land of promise. Each plague demonstrated God's might, as He used all that He created to execute the purposes and plans He desired. The final plague and God's miraculous protection of His people was reminiscent of the way He cared for Adam and Eve following their sin and provided for Abraham when he prepared to sacrifice Isaac. The firstborn son of every family in Egypt was marked for death, yet God promised to protect the children of Israelite families. Those who trusted God's word slaughtered an animal and spread its blood over the doors of their homes. When the angel came to kill the children, those who lived in homes covered by blood were spared from God's wrath. Once again, God saved those with faith in His promises, based on a blood sacrifice that died in their place.

LUKE 22:14-23

The Passover became a long-standing memorial among God's people. Each year, they commemorated the act of God's deliverance through a ceremony that was meant to remind them of the faithfulness of God to save His people. Jesus chose this occasion to gather His disciples before His crucifixion. During the ceremonial Passover meal, he told His disciples that the broken bread was a picture of what would soon happen to His body. The cup was a picture of His blood that would be spilt. The significance of the Passover would intensify through Jesus' work. No longer would it picture a past event where God delivered a specific nation from slavery in Egypt. Now all those who lived by faith in Jesus would eat the bread and drink the cup as a picture of the deliverance from slavery to sin that Jesus' death and resurrection made possible. Throughout all history, this meal, often known as the Lord's Supper, would point to Jesus' body that was broken and His blood that was poured out so that His people could be saved.

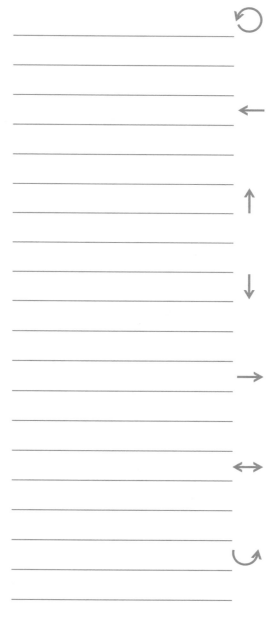

EXODUS 14

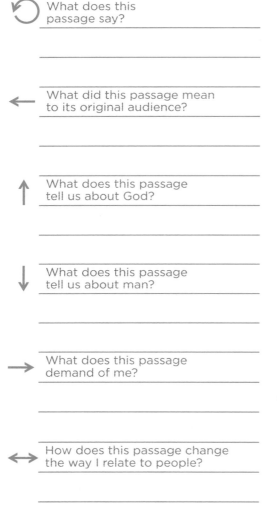

What does this passage say?

What did this passage mean to its original audience?

What does this passage tell us about God?

What does this passage tell us about man?

What does this passage demand of me?

How does this passage change the way I relate to people?

What does this passage prompt me to pray to God?

Most people, Christian and non-Christian alike, know the story told in Exodus 14. Moses led the people to freedom from slavery in Egypt. Their route of escape was miraculous—Moses divided the sea and the people walked through as if they were merely crossing on a path. Once across, the waters returned to normal and the Egyptians, who were pursuing God's people, were swallowed up by the sea. The crossing of the Red Sea was a work so mighty, so powerful, that it could only be God's doing. After the series of plagues and the miraculous deliverance through the sea, no one was tempted to think the Israelites, much less Moses, were delivered by their own efforts. They could only stand in awe of God's work and praise Him for His great salvation, which they did in the following chapter. Worship is the natural response of those who have been saved by God.

EXODUS 19:1-6

Many people falsely assume that Christianity boils down to keeping rules. We've disobeyed God by our sin, and the way to please God and rebuild our relationship with Him is by being good and living according to His standards—or so we're prone to think. No matter how hard we try, however, we find that we're just not very good at keeping His rules, at least not for very long. This is why God's grace, and not our obedience, lies at the heart of the Christian faith. But God's grace doesn't mean people are allowed to go on freely sinning. While obedience doesn't save us, it does have an important place in the life of God's people. Exodus 19 makes this clear. God points back to the salvation that He's already provided for His people and then, as a result of that grace, tells them that they should desire to obey. Through their obedience, they will be a holy nation empowered to fulfill their creation mission of reflecting God's image throughout the world. Obedience—in the life of the nation of Israel and in our lives as well—is a result of God's grace, which then compels us to accomplish the mission He's given us.

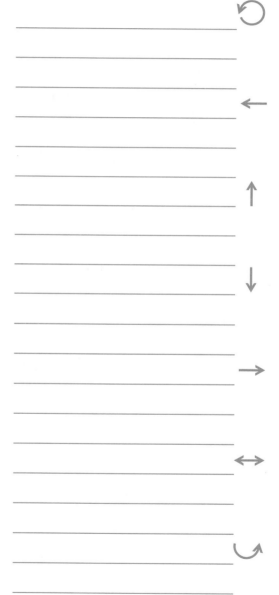

EXODUS 20:1-21

In order to help God's people obey, He gave them the law. The first Ten Commandments are summarized in Exodus 20, though the remainder of the book of Exodus and portions of the next three books continue to spell out hundreds of laws God gave His people. This helped them know what it looked like when they properly reflected His image. These rules were not random, unfair, or mean-spirited. They were actually a gift of God's grace. As their Creator, He knows how life is meant to be lived. He knows what is best for His people. He understands what will help them fulfill their mission in life. He gave them laws to protect them from those sins that would cause them great harm, as He did for Adam and Eve in the Garden. He also provided His law so that the nation would see how much they needed God's grace because, as we will soon see, the people were incapable of keeping God's holy law. They proved to be rebels from God, just like their first parents. God knew this would be the case, which is why He sent Jesus, who did what Israel could not do, perfectly keeping God's law and permanently defeating Satan.

If you wonder how long the nation of Israel would live in obedience to God, look no further than Exodus 32. While Moses was on the mountain receiving God's law, the people quickly grew frustrated and discouraged. They were a thrown together nation of former slaves trying to get to their new home. They needed leadership, yet Moses stayed on the mountain awhile talking with God. So they decided to fashion their own god, a golden statue, to worship and which they trusted to lead them to the land. They followed the pattern Paul described in Romans 1 as they exchanged the worship of God for the worship of some created thing. Adam and Eve did this in the garden. The nation of Israel did this at Mount Sinai. And you and I do this far too often. Rather than trust God and celebrate His greatness, we run to created things. No golden statue could lead the people—only the one true God could do that. He had proven His loving leadership in the past and wanted to lead them in the future, but the nation of Israel decided they had a better plan. Their rebellion once again demonstrated the deep brokenness of God's creation and how desperate they were for another act of His grace.

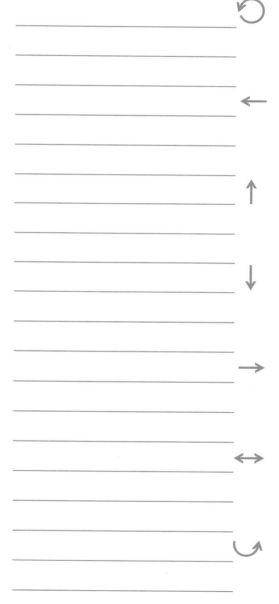

EPHESIANS 2:4-10

↺ _____
_____
_____

← _____
_____
_____

↑ _____
_____
_____

↓ _____
_____
_____

→ _____
_____
_____

↔ _____
_____
_____

↩ _____
_____
_____

The story of the nation of Israel is a story of God's grace. Nowhere along the way did the people deserve God's work on their behalf. They were sinful through and through, and the story of their slavery in Egypt is a picture of how great their sin actually was—they were trapped, weak, powerless, and dead. But God acted on their behalf and saved them for His glory. Like God's people in Egypt, all people are born dead in sin, enslaved to its power. And like the Israelites in Egypt, God's people are the recipients of His favor and kindness. In Ephesians 2:4, Paul shifts his focus away from the terrible state of humanity with these two words—"But God!" All people would be doomed to face God's wrath were it not for God's grace to provide Jesus. But God! He acts in grace to save sinners, and all we have to do is place faith in His grace gift. It seems too simple to comprehend, but this is how God works. He loves to save sinners in such a way that only He gets the glory—both sinners enslaved in Egypt long ago and sinners enslaved to sin today.

LEVITICUS 1

God saved His people from slavery and gave them His law so they could reflect Him in the world. The nation of Israel was poised to move from Mount Sinai to the land God promised Abraham, Isaac, and Jacob. Along the way, God provided them with an elaborate sacrificial system designed to deal with their sin. You may remember back in Genesis 3 when God responded to Adam and Eve's sin by clothing them with the skins of a blood sacrifice. That same pattern continues in the book of Leviticus as God instituted a system through which various types of sins could be forgiven. Though the exact nature of the sacrifices differed according to the various types of sin, there was a common theme. Sin deserves death. Either the people who sinned must die or something must die in their place. The substitute was most often a perfect, unblemished animal who would bear the sins of the people, dying in their place. You can imagine what it would be like to live in a culture where daily sacrifices were being made for sin. The smell of blood and burning flesh would be a vivid reminder that sin was costly. And this was exactly God's point.

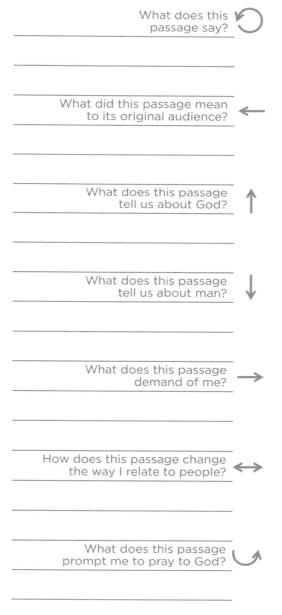

What does this passage say?

What did this passage mean to its original audience?

What does this passage tell us about God?

What does this passage tell us about man?

What does this passage demand of me?

How does this passage change the way I relate to people?

What does this passage prompt me to pray to God?

LEVITICUS 6:8-30

↺ _____

_____

_____

← _____

_____

_____

↑ _____

_____

_____

↓ _____

_____

_____

→ _____

_____

_____

↔ _____

_____

_____

↳ _____

_____

_____

God appointed one particular tribe in the nation of Israel—the Levites, descendants of Aaron—to function as priests. The role of the priests was carefully prescribed by God because it was critical for the work of the sacrificial system. Basically, the priests would play the role of the middle-man between the people and God, going to God on behalf of the people. Sinful Israelites would bring their sacrifice to the priest, who would kill it on behalf of the sinner. Before killing the animal, the priest would confess the sins of the people, symbolically transferring the sin to the animal who would die for the sin that was placed upon it. The priest would then declare God's verdict of forgiveness to the people and remind them of God's gracious favor. Because the priest would interact with God in a personal way, everything about their role was intentional—from the place of the offering and the clothes they wore to the way they disposed of the sacrifice. Later biblical authors make an astounding point regarding Jesus' work—He served as both the perfect sacrifice and the holy priest, fulfilling all of the functions of the sacrificial system completely. Today, Christians don't depend on a priest, because Jesus serves as the great, High Priest over the people of God.

LEVITICUS 16

The Day of Atonement annually reminded the Israelites of the horrific nature of sin and the necessity of a substitute. While there were always sacrifices being offered for sin, God prescribed a certain day each year when a sacrifice would be made on behalf of the whole nation. Two goats were selected—both without blemish. The priest selected one goat, confessed the sins of the people over the goat, and sent it out into the wilderness to die. The sin of the nation was also placed on the second goat, which was then killed and its blood sprinkled on the altar of God, the place of His presence among His people. These two goats pictured the work God does to forgive sinners. Like the first goat, God takes the sin of the people away— the Psalmist tells us as far as the east is from the west (Ps. 103:12). And like the second goat, He satisfies His wrath for sin by killing a substitute rather than the guilty sinner. This ceremonial day served to constantly remind the people that without the death of a substitute, it was impossible for sin to be atoned for and for people to be made right with God.

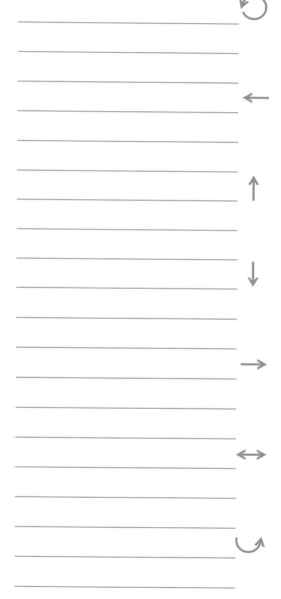

LEVITICUS 19:1-8

Holiness defines God's standard. He desires that His people pursue holiness because it reflects the essence of God. The word "holy" refers to something that is pure, spotless, without blemish. God is holy—everything about who He is and what He does in the world is absolutely perfect. There are no hidden actions, no impure motives, no falsehood or deception with God. He calls His people to reflect this holiness. In fact, that's why He created men and women in the first place. They were His image bearers—set up in the world to show off the holiness of God. God saved the nation of Israel, gave them the law and the sacrificial system, and lived among them in a special way. They would live lives marked with holiness, so that God's image would be seen in all the world. God's holy standard never changes—however, the Bible is a testimony to the fact that people living in a broken world are incapable of fulfilling of this goal. People always fall short. Therefore, if you and I are going to know God and reflect Him, it will only happen because of His grace and His Spirit's power at work in our lives.

HEBREWS 10:1-14

The author of the book of Hebrews picked up on many of the themes found in the first five books of the Bible—particularly the sacrificial system. He took various aspects of God's plan in the Old Testament and showed that Jesus was greater than every facet of the system God prescribed for the nation of Israel. In Hebrews 10, the author demonstrated that the old system for dealing with sin was inadequate because it required the priest and the people to continually offer sacrifices. He could never quit or sit down and rest from his work. The people could never stop bringing sacrifices, because as soon as they offered one substitute, they'd go out and sin again requiring another sacrifice. What they needed was a permanent atonement, which is exactly what Jesus provided. He offered Himself as a perfect sacrifice for the past, present, and future sins of His people. Once He offered His life as a substitute, the work was finished. Jesus did not have to die year after year. He was the perfect, once-and-for-all sacrifice for God's people. Those who trust in Him through faith can know that their sin is forgiven and they will never need another substitute—the perfect Lamb of God has already finished His work.

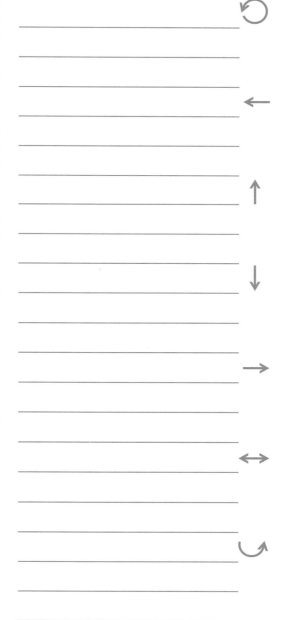

NUMBERS 1:1-19

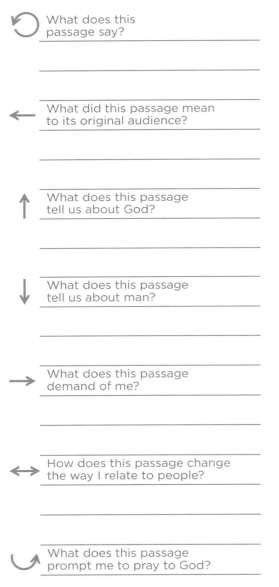

What does this passage say?

What did this passage mean to its original audience?

What does this passage tell us about God?

What does this passage tell us about man?

What does this passage demand of me?

How does this passage change the way I relate to people?

What does this passage prompt me to pray to God?

In this third chapter of God's story, we revisit a number of big themes we've already seen—God's miraculous salvation, the giving of the law, and the institution of the sacrificial system. But another critical aspect of God's promise becomes most prominent in the books of Numbers and Deuteronomy—the land. God pledged to give Abraham and his vast family a land on which they would live in safety, enjoy God's care, and shine as a light to the nations. They were set free from slavery and given everything they would need to settle in this land. The book of Numbers begins, as its name would suggest, with a count of those within each tribe in Israel. The numbers varied from tribe to tribe, but one thing was sure—God had been faithful to His promise and Israel was now a vast nation. From one childless family to twelve tribes numbering thousands upon thousands, God kept His word and the people were poised to picture Him in ways one singular person could never do. They're on the brink of living in the land, seemingly ready to worship God rightly, but sadly, we will see that although sin may obstruct God's mission, it doesn't obliterate His promises.

NUMBERS 6:1-21

The Nazarite vow was a special promise certain men made to indicate their commitment to a distinct form of holiness. Their role within the nation of Israel was unclear, yet their holy life was a symbol of God's calling on all His people. The commitments made by those who took the Nazarite vow showed that holiness was concrete— it involved real life commitments that marked someone as distinct in the world. Holiness has practical implications for the lives of God's people which can be observed by others. This is true throughout God's story. His people, saved by His grace, are called to live distinctly holy lives that others can see. This holy life isn't pursued in an effort to earn God's favor or point praise to the holy people themselves. Rather, holy lives are meant to be a reflection and response to God's grace pointing others to His glory.

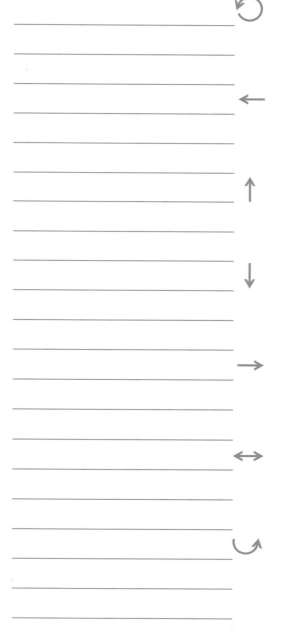

NUMBERS 9:15-23

↻ _____

_____

_____

← _____

_____

_____

↑ _____

_____

_____

↓ _____

_____

_____

→ _____

_____

_____

↔ _____

_____

_____

↱ _____

_____

_____

God actively led His people from their release in Egypt to the promised land. His work was vividly seen in their deliverance from Egypt as He demonstrated His might and power through the plagues and the crossing of the Red Sea. Once the nation was free, God continued to manifest His leadership in the form of a cloud during the day and fire by night. The visible demonstration of the presence of God provided clear guidance as to when they were to move and in what direction they were to go. As the people would soon learn, they were wholly dependent on God's leadership. It would be deadly for the people to move without His presence. So long as they followed His leading and moved when and how He directed, they would be assured of smooth passage. The submission of the nation to the leadership of God proves a pattern for all of God's people who seek to follow Him on His mission in the world.

NUMBERS 11:1-15

It's fascinating to see how quickly the nation began to grumble against God and Moses. Not so long ago, they were crushed under the weight of slavery in Egypt. But they were freed. God brought them safely out of slavery and guided them to a land He'd promised would be exceedingly wonderful. He also fed them with food they had never seen and did not deserve. The people, much like us, were quick to forget God's faithfulness and blessing. They looked back on their previous life with fond memories and complained about their present situation, questioning God's goodness and Moses' leadership. God, once again, acted in judgment to remind the people that He was at work to care for them and bring them into the land of promise. Rather than grumbling about what they lacked, they should have celebrated God's blessings and trusted that He had their best interest at heart.

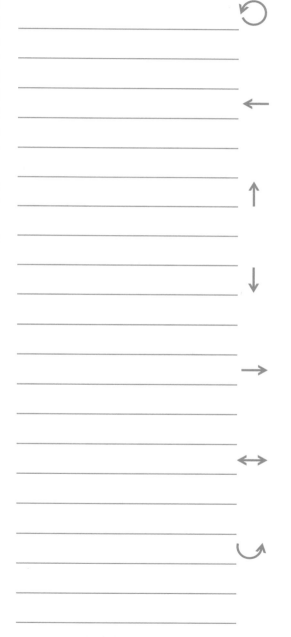

JOHN 6:22-59

↻ _____

_____

_____

← _____

_____

_____

↑ _____

_____

_____

↓ _____

_____

_____

→ _____

_____

_____

↔ _____

_____

_____

↱ _____

_____

_____

Jesus used many word pictures to communicate who He was and what He was on the earth to accomplish. The Gospel of John is filled with stories in which Jesus took a concept that would have been familiar to the people and used that image to help people understand His work. For example, in John 10, Jesus compared His mission to that of a shepherd caring for his sheep. Here Jesus uses the imagery of bread, particularly the manna God provided for His people in the Old Testament. God sent Jesus as a true and lasting form of food, the kind that would satisfy not simply physical hunger, but spiritual hunger as well. Like the Israelites, the Jewish people of Jesus' day grumbled at this description because Jesus had equated Himself with God's salvation. In other words, he said that He was the one that could meet their spiritual needs and save their souls. No one but God could say something like that. To those who were not God's people this news provoked grumbling—but to God's people, it brought great joy!

NUMBERS 13:25–14:1

God faithfully brought the Israelites to the brink of the promised land. When they arrived, they noticed that the land was already filled with inhabitants. And not just any inhabitants—the people who filled the land were intimidating and strong. Moses and Aaron sent twelve spies into the land to assess the situation, and their report did not inspire confidence. The land was a good land, filled with the blessings of God just as He has said, but the people who lived there were impressive, and their cities were big and well protected. The group of former slaves cowered anxiously on the outskirts of the land, unsure how they would ever live in the promised land. Two spies, Caleb and Joshua, still believed that the people could take the land, but the rest of the nation did not agree. They rebelled, making decisions based on fear rather than faith. They even sought out a leader to take them back to slavery in Egypt. God's anger burned against the people, and He reminded them through Joshua and Caleb that what was most important wasn't the size or power of the enemy, but the presence of God. If He is with us, we have nothing to fear—a lesson the Israelites had seen time and time.

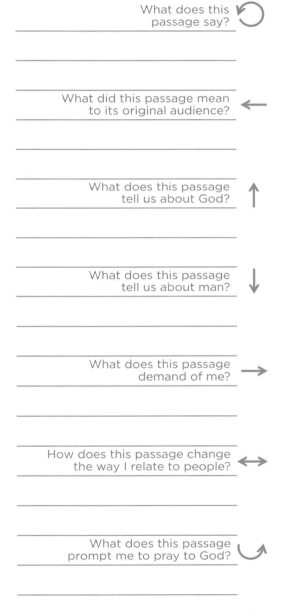

What does this passage say?

What did this passage mean to its original audience?

What does this passage tell us about God?

What does this passage tell us about man?

What does this passage demand of me?

How does this passage change the way I relate to people?

What does this passage prompt me to pray to God?

DAY 72

NUMBERS 14:13-38

We are right back where we were in the early stages of the book of Genesis. Though a lot of time had passed, God's image-bearers were still rebelling against His guidance and grace. God had every right to wipe them out and destroy His creation as He did in the flood, but Moses begged God to relent, pointing out that the nations would see the destruction of Israel and assume that God was not powerful enough to bring them into the land. Moses pointed to God's gracious character—that He is slow to anger and abounding in steadfast love. This phrase became common throughout the Old Testament. God is not like you and me. He does not grow weary or fail to keep His promises of love. He loves consistently, even though people are often highly unlovable. Yet God is also just. Because of the people's sin, the entire generation that was delivered from slavery in Egypt would not live in the promised land—they would die in the wilderness, never stepping foot in the land. Once again, we see God's promises will not be thwarted—He would keep His promise by allowing their children to enter the land instead.

NUMBERS 20:1-13

The ever-grumbling Israelites muttered and complained once again. They'd been cast out into the wilderness, where they would wander until the entire first generation died. The heat was scorching and the people lacked sufficient water, and God could have chosen to allow them to die in the wilderness. But as we will see, He instead taught some important lessons during their years in the wilderness. He graciously cared for them by providing manna for food and water to drink. Moses and Aaron were used to care for and lead God's people, and in this case, they were to do so by speaking to a rock from which God would provide water. However, Moses, likely frustrated by the sin of the people and questioning the provision of God, did not speak to the rock as God had instructed. Instead, Moses struck the rock—a grave mistake. God graciously provided the water He'd promised. Because of Moses' failure to carefully obey God's instruction, he would die with the rest of the generation. It's essential that we always follow God, trusting in His power instead of acting in our own strength.

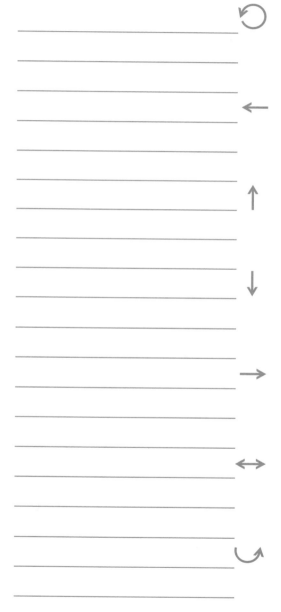

DAY 74

NUMBERS 21:4-9

↺ _____

_____

_____

← _____

_____

_____

↑ _____

_____

_____

↓ _____

_____

_____

→ _____

_____

_____

↔ _____

_____

_____

↪ _____

_____

_____

The rampant sin of the people was met, time and again, with God's judgment. This time, He judged the people by sending serpents which would bite and kill many. The death of the people at the teeth of the serpents was an eerie reminder of the death of their first parents, Adam and Eve. Once again, God provided a way of escape. Moses constructed an image of a serpent and lifted it up on a pole in the midst of the people. Those who looked to the bronze serpent would live, and those who did not would die. This is not exactly the way you'd expect God to heal someone from a snake bite. No medicine. No doctors. The people were to simply trust in faith, the God-appointed way of salvation. The only way to be spared from death was to follow the plan God created, no matter how extraordinarily strange it seemed.

JOHN 3:1-21

At the beginning of Jesus' earthly ministry, He described God's plan for salvation to a religious leader named Nicodemus. Nicodemus was a direct descendant of God's people in the Old Testament and would have been well-versed in all aspects of religious behavior. He was confident in his understanding of the ways God would save His people. But Jesus challenged His assumptions, declaring that salvation was possible when someone was born again through faith in Jesus' work. This understanding of salvation would have been as unlikely as the use of a bronze serpent in Numbers 21. Jesus used this story to remind Nicodemus that this nonsensical type of plan for salvation was exactly what God had been orchestrating throughout His story. Soon Jesus would be lifted up, not as a serpent on a pole, but as a Savior on a cross, and all those who looked to Him in faith would be saved.

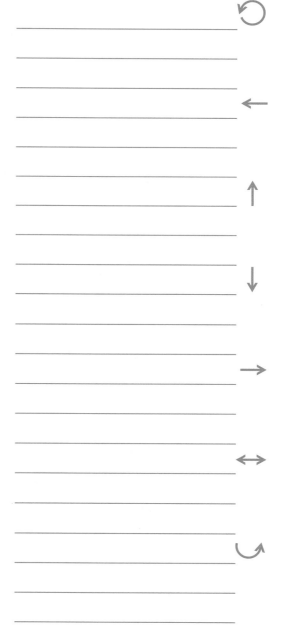

DEUTERONOMY 2:1-25

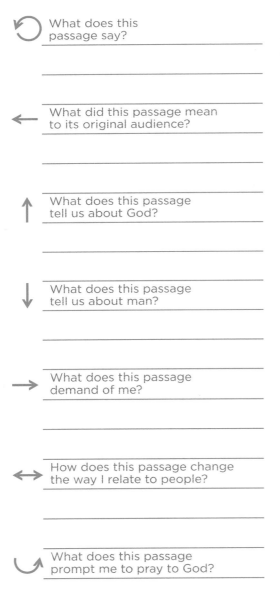

What does this passage say?

_____

_____

What did this passage mean to its original audience?

_____

_____

What does this passage tell us about God?

_____

_____

What does this passage tell us about man?

_____

_____

What does this passage demand of me?

_____

_____

How does this passage change the way I relate to people?

_____

_____

What does this passage prompt me to pray to God?

_____

_____

Israel spent 40 years in the wilderness as a punishment for their sin. God, who is always faithful to His promises, did not abandon His people. Always present with them during their wandering, He fed them with food they did not deserve and provided personal guidance and protection. God's promises were fulfilled when the second-generation, and not the first, would take the promised land. Moses would also not enter the land, so the book of Deuteronomy recounted several of his sermons as the people gazed at the land they were attempting to take for the second time. Moses' counsel began with a reminder that God never, not for a moment, abandoned His people. His presence was with them and would continue to go with them as they journeyed into the land. Faith in God's power and protection was the most essential ingredient in successfully taking the land and dwelling there as a nation of image-bearers.

DEUTERONOMY 4:1-14

The statutes and rules of God were not random or purposeless. Moses reminded the people that God's laws had an inward and outward motive. Inwardly, the people's obedience to God was the path to life. Life means more than just physical survival, though it certainly includes that. It also includes the ability to thrive—to enjoy all of God's blessings. God knows how life is best lived, and obedience to His Word is the way to enjoy God and His world. God's rules also included an outward dimension. The holiness of the people was intended to reflect outwardly to the surrounding nations. Others were meant to look at God's people and see men and women marked by holiness. Their distinct lives should point others to God and His glory.

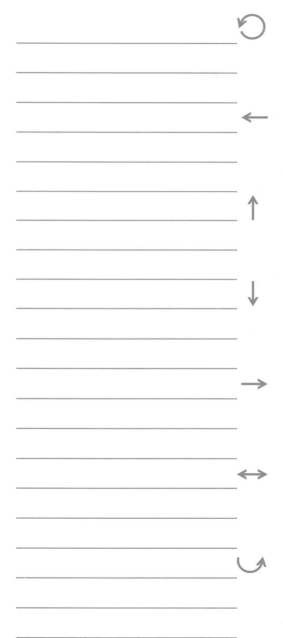

DEUTERONOMY 6:1-15

↻ _____

_____

_____

← _____

_____

_____

↑ _____

_____

_____

↓ _____

_____

_____

→ _____

_____

_____

↔ _____

_____

_____

↩ _____

_____

_____

God acts graciously toward His people. He proved, time and again, that He would fulfill His promises in spite of the people's sin. At this point, they were ready to enter the promised land. Moses reminded them of the critical role leaders, especially parents, play in teaching others about God's character and works. This was, and is, the mechanism that God established to make sure following generations know God. The family is meant to be a community that reminds one another of God's glory. The loss of the knowledge of God is always only one generation away. Sadly, many grow up in homes with parents who either don't know the Lord or who fail to prioritize Him in their lives. In your life, you should praise God for the ways He has revealed Himself to you. If you have parents who love God and love you enough to point you to Him, praise God specifically for this blessing!

DEUTERONOMY 8

Moses revealed to the nation the reason for their 40 years in the wilderness. Not only had God been with them, but He had also been at work in their hearts to prepare them for their second attempt to enter the land. Before, the people chose to trust in their own wisdom—the inhabitants were powerful and the cites intimidating so they thought there was no hope for success. God judged by sending them into the wilderness to humble them and teach them that they were entirely dependent on Him for victory. This was why the inhabitants of the land were intimidating in the first place—the whole purpose was that God's people would take the land only by God's power. Forty years later, they should be in a much better position to appreciate this reality. They'd been forced to learn to depend on God, and they would put that dependence to the test.

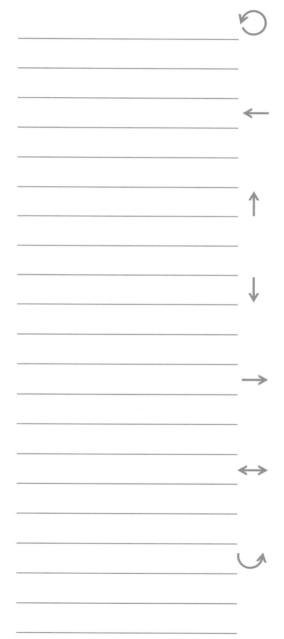

MATTHEW 4:1-17

○ _____

← _____

↑ _____

↓ _____

→ _____

↔ _____

↺ _____

Jesus quoted Deuteronomy more than any other Old Testament book. Jesus launched His public ministry by confronting the temptations of Satan in the wilderness. Unlike Adam and Eve and the nation of Israel, Jesus stood firm in the face of temptation and obeyed God rather than submit to Satan's schemes. Jesus' 40 days in the wilderness modeled the 40 years the rebellious people spent wandering in the wilderness. It's no wonder that Jesus used Scripture taken from Deuteronomy 8 to confront Satan! Because He was God, Jesus understood that dependence on the Father was better than any substitute. Where Adam and Israel failed, Jesus succeeded in faithfully fulfilling His mission in the world because He was the exact imprint of the image of God. Those who live in faith learn to fight Satan's temptations through God's Word and dependence on Father.

DEUTERONOMY 9:1-5

God reminded His people of their national history by first pointing their attention away from themselves and to the power of God. He knew the people would be tempted to assume they were given the land because of something they had done. Specifically, God cautioned them against assuming they deserved the land because of their moral uprightness. The opposite was actually true—the people did not model consistent godliness, and they had not always kept the law. God granted the land to them as a pure act of grace. The same temptation awaits all of those who have faith in Jesus today. It is easy to think we did something right to deserve God's good gifts—our family, friends, food, work, and health. We can even begin to think that we deserve our salvation due to our ability keep God's law, especially when we compare ourselves with the failures of those around us. We can be tempted to think we're better than others and deserve God's favor. Israel's story is a reminder to us all that everything we have is a gift of God's grace and not the result of our goodness.

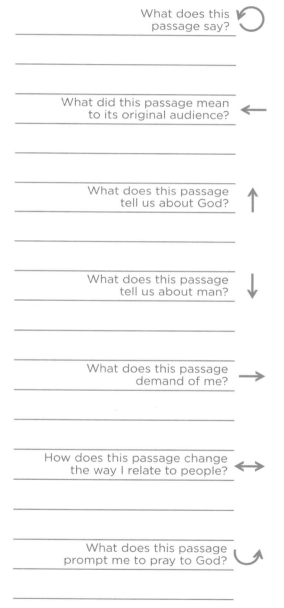

What does this passage say?

What did this passage mean to its original audience?

What does this passage tell us about God?

What does this passage tell us about man?

What does this passage demand of me?

How does this passage change the way I relate to people?

What does this passage prompt me to pray to God?

DEUTERONOMY 11:26-32

Two mountains served as an ever-present reminder to God's people once they entered the land. On one mountain, Mount Gerizim, they created a memorial to the blessings of God. And on the other, Mount Ebal, they built a reminder to God's curses. Each mountain reminded them of the clear instructions of God. If they obeyed God's Word in the land, they would experience His blessings. If they disobeyed Him, they would experience His curse. The primary way the people disobeyed was by worshiping the false gods found among the inhabitants of the land. They had already been freed from slavery, given the law, experienced God's presence, and soon they would be in the land. Each of these steps was the clear result of God's grace which should have propelled the people toward obedience. They should have obeyed as a response to God's grace and were further warned about the consequences of disobeying. Christians today do not obey in order to experience salvation, but once we've been saved, we seek to obey God as a response to His grace. As we obey, we find that God's ways are a path to life and blessing, and that following after sin only leads to destruction.

DEUTERONOMY 21:22-23

The middle chapters of the book of Deuteronomy repeat much of what has already been said to the people. As Moses neared death, he took the opportunity to remind the nation of God's care and commandments. They could look back over their history and see God's faithful care time and time again. At the top of the list of evidences of God's grace was the law—commands issued from God regarding virtually every aspect of the lives of His people. Many of these commands discussed how sin should have been handled by the nation, such as how murderers or thieves should be treated. Those who committed a heinous crime were to be punished by death. If the individual was hanged, Moses warned, the nation should not leave the body hanging from the tree overnight. Rather, the person should be buried quickly so that the good land God provided would not be cursed with dead bodies. Later biblical authors would pick up on this picture and apply it to Jesus, who took on God's curse for human sin by dying on a cross.

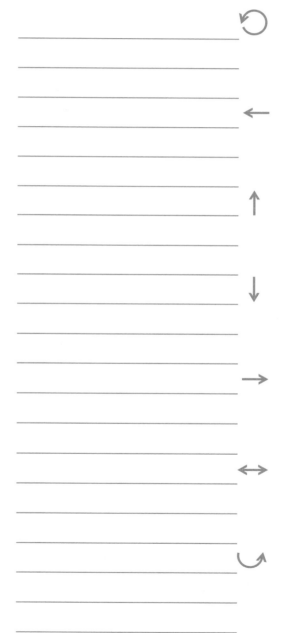

DEUTERONOMY 30

↺ _____

_____

← _____

_____

↑ _____

_____

↓ _____

_____

→ _____

_____

↔ _____

_____

↪ _____

_____

God knew of the future failure of His people. The history of God's image-bearers shows that people have a track record of disobedience. It doesn't seem to matter how powerful God has been or what He has done. His people still rebel. That's why the book of Deuteronomy ends with a discussion of repentance and forgiveness. God promised that He would forgive the sins of the people if they simply recognized their error, turned from their sin, and trusted His Word. He did not minimize the pain caused by sin and warned that sin could mean the people would lose the land. Just as God gave the land to the Israelites as a blessing, He could remove them from the land as a curse. If this happened (and it did), God made it clear that this punishment would not be forever. All the nation needed to do was repent, and God would establish them on the land once again, just as He would do after their 40 years of wandering in the wilderness. Sin will never have the final word—God's grace will.

HEBREWS 3

You can imagine that the nation of Israel revered Moses by the time of his death. They had certainly grumbled, complained, and rebelled against his leadership, yet it was Moses who led them to freedom and brought them to the edge of the promised land twice. Once they entered the land and Moses died, it became clear to the people how great Moses had been and all that he had done on their behalf. The writer of Hebrews didn't deny the greatness of Moses, but he did say that Jesus is even greater than Moses. Why? Moses was merely a man used by God to do many great things, whereas Jesus was God who had the power in Himself to do far greater things. Jesus gives His people true rest—something Moses could not do in his life, and something the people would never truly find in the land, at least not for long. Jesus' great work means that all people should turn to Him in faith and follow His ways. All people should trust Him to lead, rather than hardening their hearts as the Israelites did in the wilderness. Through Jesus, we can find the rest our sin-weary souls long for.

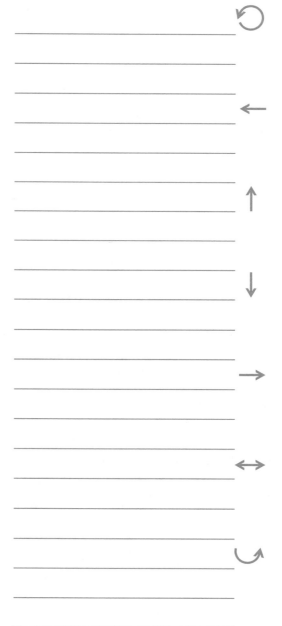

CHAPTER 4//PEOPLE

The fourth chapter of God's story narrates the way God's people entered and inhabited the promised land. This chapter feels long overdue. All the way back in Genesis 12, Abram was promised a land for himself and his descendants. The story, from that point to the beginning of the Book of Joshua, is packed with twists and turns to say the least. Successes and failures, key leaders and complaining people, and seemingly random laws and important promises fill their history.

The story of Israel is much like our story. Because we live in a sin-drenched world, the circumstances of our lives are often not what we'd expect. Imagine that you sat down to write your entire life story when you were 10 years old. What events would you include? Would you mention your first car, getting a job, graduating from high school, or moving away for college? What would you leave out of your story? What types of pain would you assume you'd never experience?

Each of us could probably construct a life-story we wish we could live. The problem is we will never live out our life story exactly as we might imagine. If you fast-forward to your thirtieth birthday, you will certainly find all sorts of twists and turns that you would have never imagined. Some of these diversions might come to you at no fault of your own. We live in a world where people get cancer, parents divorce, and friends move away to new cities. These experiences, and others like them, can change the course of our lives in significant ways.

At other times, life changes occur because we make bad decisions. Like we've seen throughout the Bible, all humans are born in a state of sin that causes them to do all sorts of foolish things. People make bad choices, desire the things this world offers, and rebel from God. Thinking we know best, we choose a path that leads to destruction.

Combined, these forces alter the direction of our lives time and again. That's why it's important that we see God's faithfulness as the backdrop of the entire story of the Bible. In spite of the sin of the people and the brokenness of the world, He is still faithful to fulfill His promises. He can, and does, work through sin to bring about His good purposes in the lives of His people. In this chapter of God's story, told through the Books of Joshua, Judges, and Ruth, we will see the ever-present hand of God orchestrating all things so that His glory is revealed.

JOSHUA 1:1-9

God appointed Joshua to lead the people of Israel following the death of Moses. The book bearing his name begins with a call to action. The second generation of those who escaped from Egypt were ready to take the land. What's interesting about the conquest of the promised land is that God had already pledged to give the people the land! This inescapable outcome was like watching a football game you've recorded when you already know the final score. God's people would certainly inherit the land—all they needed to do was trust God, keep His commandments, and have confidence in His promises. The strength and courage Joshua called them to was not based on the might or power of the nation, but on the glory of God. Since He was all-powerful, they had nothing to fear if they would simply do what He said.

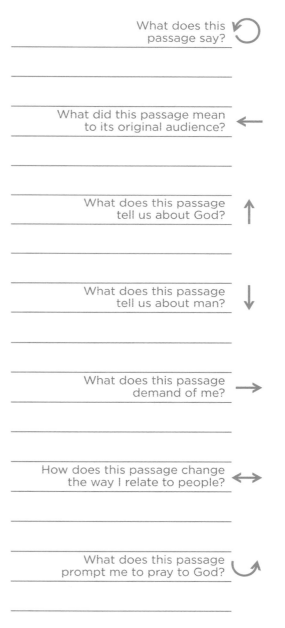

What does this passage say?

What did this passage mean to its original audience?

What does this passage tell us about God?

What does this passage tell us about man?

What does this passage demand of me?

How does this passage change the way I relate to people?

What does this passage prompt me to pray to God?

DAY 87

JOSHUA 3:9-17

↺ _____
_____
_____
← _____
_____
_____
↑ _____
_____
↓ _____
_____
_____
→ _____
_____
_____
↔ _____
_____
_____
↻ _____
_____
_____

Have you noticed, when reading the story of the nation of Israel, it's God who wrote the story? Each step along the way suggests scenes of the past and points forward to the coming of Jesus Christ, who serves as the fulfillment of all of God's promises in the Old Testament. The Jordan River stood as the natural border between the wilderness, where God's people were, and the promised land where they were going. The priests led the way across the Jordan while carrying the ark of the covenant, which held the commandments from God and was the symbol of His presence with His people. Just as at the Red Sea, the priests entered the river and God separated the water making a dry path on which the people could cross. They were delivered from slavery through a divided sea and now they stepped into the land of God's blessing by crossing a divided river. Grace upon grace, indeed.

JOSHUA 6

The story of the fall of Jericho is very familiar to many people. It often makes its way into children's Bible storybooks and songs. It represents a defining moment for the nation of Israel, as well as a vivid picture of God's power at work on behalf of His people. The city of Jericho was important for Israel since it sat on the edge of the promised land, and the inhabitants of the city were the first that Israel would drive out of the land. It is clear from the tactics God used to destroy Jericho that He was ensuring the glory from any victory would go to Him and not to Israel. No military strategist would have drawn up this battle plan—marching around a city, blowing trumpets, and shouting seemed like a strange approach indeed. That is, unless you understand the point. God ensured the credit for the victory went to Him, and He desired that the outcome of the victory would result in His people trusting Him. Since they followed the strange battle plan and trusted God, the city was destroyed and Israel was victorious. If only they would continue to follow this pattern over and over again, they would certainly drive out the inhabitants in the land and live in safety.

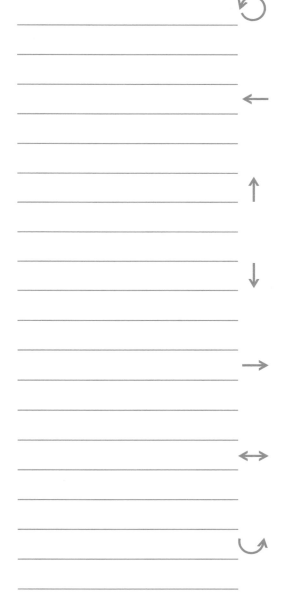

JOSHUA 8:30-35

↻ _____

_____

← _____

_____

_____

↑ _____

_____

_____

↓ _____

_____

_____

→ _____

_____

_____

↔ _____

_____

_____

↪ _____

_____

_____

Now occupying the land, Joshua led the people to renew their commitment to God and His Word. You should notice that everything the people did was exactly what God had already told them to do. They offered sacrifices on an altar in the land, they plastered the blessings and curses on two mountains, they even read the law in the presence of all the people, calling one another to obedience. They began this new stage in the nation's story with obedience and worship. This scene, combined with the fall of Jericho, provides the framework for what we should expect to continue reading in the coming books, that is, if the people keep their promises and walk faithfully with God. They trusted God in battle and were victorious. As they continued faithfully keeping His Word, they experienced God's blessings in this new land. Trust and obedience are to be the defining characteristics of God's people, both in the time of the nation of Israel and in our day as well.

EPHESIANS 6:10-20

You don't see Christians in our day fighting to take possession of a land God has promised, but we do live in a daily battle. Paul, writing to the church in Ephesus, made it clear that our fight is not against other people, but against Satan and his work on the earth. We wrestle against our own sin, so that we can reflect the image of God to the nations. We also fight against sin's effects in our world—starvation, abuse, modern day slavery, and homelessness are a few examples of the ways sin affects others in our world. As Christians, we should work to care for the poor and the marginalized in humanity. How do we fight sin in our lives and our world? Paul told us that we should put on the armor of God. This armor consists of faith and trust in God and in the power of His Word. Like at Jericho, this battle plan may seem strange, but if we live in dependence on God's Word, trusting His power, we can fight victoriously.

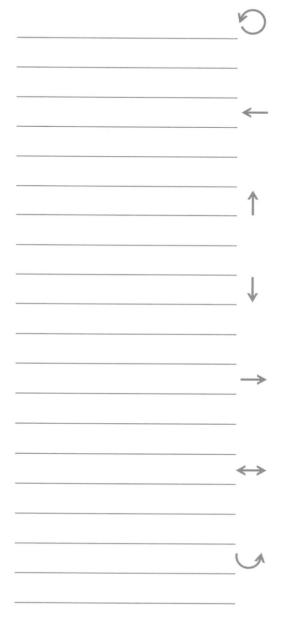

JOSHUA 13:1-7

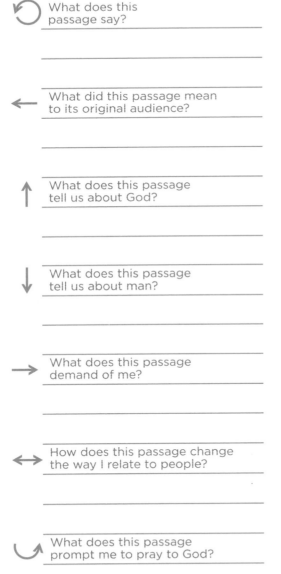

What does this
passage say?

_____

_____

_____

What did this passage mean
to its original audience?

_____

_____

What does this passage
tell us about God?

_____

_____

What does this passage
tell us about man?

_____

_____

What does this passage
demand of me?

_____

_____

How does this passage change
the way I relate to people?

_____

_____

What does this passage
prompt me to pray to God?

_____

_____

Joshua described the continuing process of taking the land. Although the people had moved into the land, it remained far from settled. Enemies still lived there, and the people were not spreading out to live throughout the area God had provided for them. So Joshua did two things. First, he divided the land among the twelves tribes of the nation—giving a certain allotment to each tribe based on its size. He then instructed these tribes to drive out the inhabitants in the land. They were not to coexist with the people who worshiped other gods—they should drive them out completely. This two-fold plan proves true for all God's people, even those living today. We, too, make every effort to drive out sin from our lives and from our world while learning to love and treasure God's good blessings in our lives. We rest in God's care and work in our lives, while also working to reflect God's image everywhere we go.

JOSHUA 21:43-45

These three simple verses serve to summarize so much of what we've read up to this point. God made promises to His people, and He was faithful to see these promises through to completion. Nothing He promised failed to happen. As the sun rose each morning and the people woke up preparing for a new day, they would see the land before them and be reminded of the steadfast love of God. Their days were intended to be filled with rest. Be careful here—when we think of rest, we often think of a long nap on the couch or sleeping in on Saturday morning. This is not what God had in mind. The people would still engage in good and meaningful work in the land. Like Adam and Eve in the garden, the blessing of God included meaningful work for His people. For Israel, rest meant that they would be free to enjoy God's blessings, live in peace with their neighbors, and be free to spend their lives serving God's purposes.

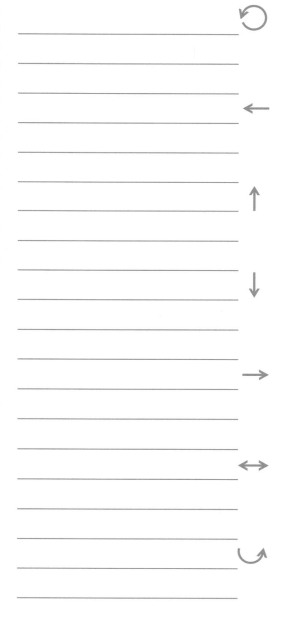

JOSHUA 24:14-28

Before his death, Joshua called the people to one of two positions. Though much to this point had been made of the nation as a whole, Joshua made the commandments of God personal to each family. He said that each family had one of two points to which they should aim. They could turn from God and serve the false gods of the nations. However, to do so would be to invite God's curse upon them, and as God had already promised, they would be driven out of the good land. The alternative was to remain faithful to God, follow Him, and teach future generations to do the same. Twice, the people affirmed their commitment to follow the one, true and living God, who had delivered them from slavery and led them to the land. Joshua took the people's own words and set up a stone to remind them of their promise. If, in the future, the people became disobedient to God, this stone would be a reminder of their pledge. Any consequences they experienced would be the direct result of poor choices.

JUDGES 1:27-36

One of the most helpful ways to understand the main point of the Bible is to notice ideas that are repeated. Remember, the Bible was written before we could add bold fonts or ten exclamation marks behind important points. All the authors had were words, so they repeated the ideas they wanted to emphasize. The book of Judges opens with such repetition. The writer named a certain tribe and then said that this tribe had not driven out the inhabitants of the land. In a clear act of rebellion, the Israelites decided to allow certain people to live alongside them in the land, even enlisting some of these foreigners to help them build cities—these former slaves started acting like slave masters. We don't know all the reasons they failed to drive out the people— maybe it was too hard or maybe they minimized (in their minds) the harm that could come if they allowed the people to stay. But what we do know is that Israel failed to obey God, and they would surely suffer the consequences.

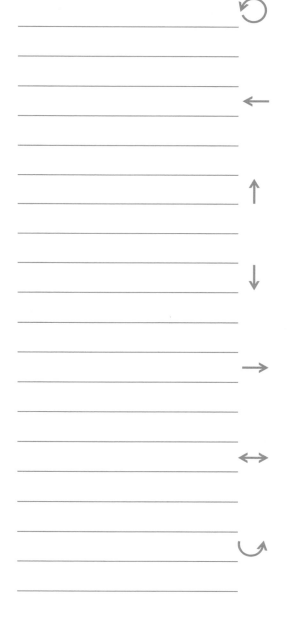

HEBREWS 4:1-13

↺ _____

_____

← _____

_____

↑ _____

_____

↓ _____

_____

→ _____

_____

↔ _____

_____

↪ _____

_____

The rest Israel experienced was short-lived. They invited disaster by allowing the foreign nations to remain in the land. The writer of Hebrews used this failure to point out yet another way that Jesus is greater. The rest that Joshua could provide for the people didn't last, but the rest Jesus gives His people lasts forever. Jesus calls people to come to Him when we are tired and burdened by the cares of life because He will provide the rest we've always wanted. Faith in Jesus provides rest because it reminds us that we do not have to work to earn God's love—salvation is a gift. We know our sins are atoned for and that we will spend eternity with God and His people in heaven. We can rest in these promises in a far greater way than the nation of Israel could rest in the land. God warned that their disobedience would bring disaster, but Christians do not have to fear the curse of God because Jesus has already absorbed God's wrath on our behalf.

JUDGES 2:6-10

At this point, the second generation, including many who were born during Israel's wilderness years, was gone. The third generation was born in the promised land and they were the recipients of God's blessings in a way the previous generations had only dreamed of. The problem was that this new generation did not know the Lord, nor did they experience the work He'd done for their parents and grandparents. It's hard to imagine how this could happen. It's not like the Red Sea could be quickly forgotten, and many in the nation probably still partly remembered these stories. When the biblical authors use the word "forget," they often mean that something no longer has an effect on your actions. This third generation no longer cared about God or what He thought of their lifestyle. The tragic tale of the book of Judges describes what happens when people forget about God.

What does this passage say?

What did this passage mean to its original audience?

What does this passage tell us about God?

What does this passage tell us about man?

What does this passage demand of me?

How does this passage change the way I relate to people?

What does this passage prompt me to pray to God?

DAY 97

JUDGES 2:11-23

↺ _____

_____

← _____

_____

↑ _____

_____

↓ _____

_____

→ _____

_____

↔ _____

_____

↰ _____

_____

God did exactly as He'd promised. The Israelites allowed the inhabitants to remain in the land, and just as God warned, they turned the hearts of Israel away from the true God. Israel began to worship idols, and as a result, the people experienced constant fighting and pain. Their distress rivaled that of their forefathers in Egypt who lived miserable lives as slaves. This time, their pain was caused by their failure to trust God and do what He said. They invited the pain that led to their destruction. God could have destroyed the nation forever, and He certainly had every reason to do so. But He didn't. Instead, He raised up judges who delivered the people from their enemies. In fact, that's exactly the role these judges played—they're not like our judges who give verdicts in court. Rather, they were people who acted on behalf of God to judge the nations and deliver God's people. The book of Judges tells the story of a series of these judges.

JUDGES 10:6-18

The book of Judges, much of the Old Testament in fact, follows a similar pattern. You might think of it as a big cycle. First, the people rebel from God. Then, they experience the consequences of their sin. After some time, they repent for their sin and cry out to God because of the pain they have experienced. God, then, gives them grace in the form of a restored relationship. Each time this pattern happens, the sin gets worse and the consequences more severe. God used judges like Gideon to work on His behalf. Gideon led a tiny army to defeat an imposing foe. Once again, God wanted to make it clear that any victory the people achieved was not based on their power or even their faithfulness, but was a sheer act of grace. Gideon reminds us that, even in the face of sin, God uses men and women to lead God's people. If God can use weak and frail sinners like Gideon, then surely He can use people like us as well.

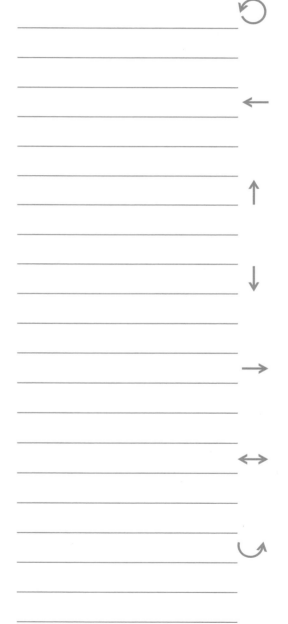

JUDGES 16

Samson's story sadly testifies to the consequences of sin. God warned Israel that they would be tempted to intermarry with the women of the surrounding nations. And if they did, they'd be drawn to worship false gods. This fundamental reality reveals a truth about all human relationships. We tend to become like those we spend the most time around. They rub off on us—either their positive virtues draw us to pursue God or their sinful actions lead us to rebel. We'd all like to think that we are somehow strong enough to resist the power of these influences, but this is simply not the case. No one is strong enough to resist the pull of the relationships that surround us, not even Samson. Even though God used him to deliver the Israelites from their Philistine enemies, He did so in spite of Samson and not because of Samson's faithfulness. This story could have been different had Samson, and all the people, simply listened to God and separated themselves from the influences of the foreign nations. As Christians, we also must consider the impact others have on our lives, and we must form deep friendships and relationships with those who will push us toward faithfulness to God and His Word.

LUKE 4:16-22

It's easy to lose sight of the main point of the Bible as we move further into the Old Testament. God promised that a child from the tribe of Judah would emerge and defeat Satan, sin, and death. Further, He would permanently deliver God's people. The sin of Israel made the promises hard to see, like trying to spot a distant mountain on a foggy day. We clearly see the people's trouble. Time and time again, sin trapped them in situations they couldn't escape. Yet we saw God acting to deliver His people, which built confidence in the fact that a lasting, permanent deliverer would come one day. And this was exactly what Jesus claimed when He inaugurated His public ministry by reading from the book of Isaiah. The deliverance He offered would be far deeper, more profound, and longer lasting than any judge could ever bring about.

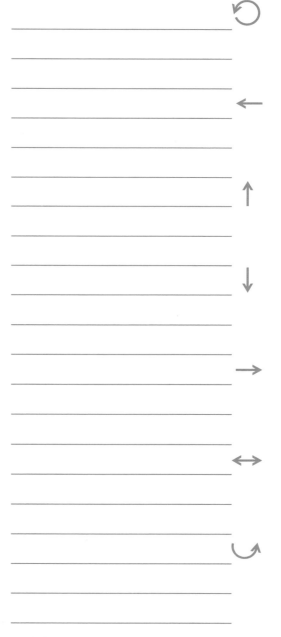

RUTH 1

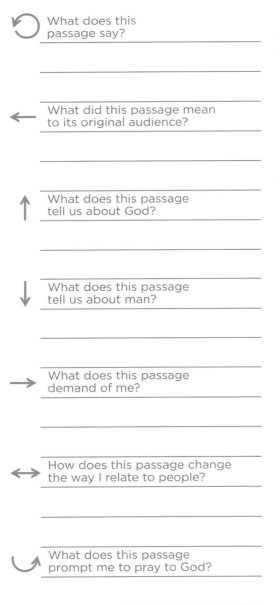

What does this passage say?

_____

_____

What did this passage mean to its original audience?

_____

_____

What does this passage tell us about God?

_____

_____

What does this passage tell us about man?

_____

_____

What does this passage demand of me?

_____

_____

How does this passage change the way I relate to people?

_____

_____

What does this passage prompt me to pray to God?

_____

_____

The book of Judges tells the frightful story of the decline of God's people and the fracturing of a nation. It ends with people who have forgotten God doing whatever they want. God continuously provided deliverers, yet the people's rebellion only intensified. Would God give up on them altogether? We learn the answer to this question in a classic Old Testament love story. The book of Ruth opens with a family in crisis. Not only do they lack food, but each of the men introduced in the beginning of the story dies, leaving Naomi, their wife and mother, and her daughter-in-law Ruth to fend for themselves. The women traveled back to Naomi's home in search of food and in hope of finding someone who would take them in as family. Their story serves as a picture of the way God loves and cares for His children. Even in the midst of their messy lives, God had not abandoned Naomi and Ruth, but worked on their behalf to provide for their needs and restore their relationships.

RUTH 2

Boaz personifies the love of God. In order to care for widows, God set up a system in which the closest male relative was responsible for bringing a widow into his family in order to meet her needs. This person was known as a kinsman-redeemer. The hope for a single woman in that day was bleak, so Naomi and Ruth desperately needed a relative of Elimelech, Naomi's deceased husband, to serve as their kinsman-redeemer. What Ruth didn't know, at this point in the story anyway, was that the field where she worked belonged to the very person who could be her redeemer. Boaz went out of his way to provide enough food for Ruth and Naomi and took notice of Ruth's work ethic in his field. Even as an outsider, a Moabite woman, God positioned Ruth in just the right way to provide for her deepest needs. Like Ruth, we can trust that, even when life doesn't make sense or seems out of control, God works on our behalf to keep His promises in ways we might never expect.

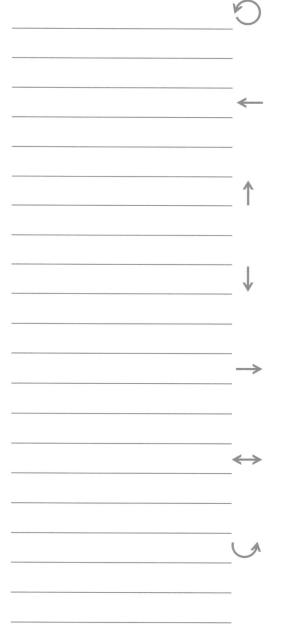

RUTH 3

Naomi developed a plan for Ruth to make it clear that these two ladies needed the redemption Boaz could provide. We've seen the language of redemption already in our Bible— the word "redeem" refers to buying something back, often concerning a position of desperation. The Israelites were redeemed from slavery in Egypt and were brought back into relationship with God. In the same way, Boaz had the opportunity to redeem Naomi and Ruth from their poverty and oppression. Neither Ruth nor Naomi could redeem themselves. Rather, they depended on someone else to work on their behalf. They were entirely at the mercy of the redeemer. If Boaz chose to show them kindness, they would be saved. If he didn't, they were doomed. All Ruth could do was cry out for help.

RUTH 4

Boaz was an honorable man. First, he offered the right of redemption to a relative with first rights to redeem Naomi and Ruth. After this man declined, Boaz willingly claimed his right of redemption, and he and Ruth married. So much happened in Ruth and Naomi's lives—for years they were hopeless, but in just a few days' events, God took a hopeless situation and proved to be capable of restoring broken lives. This tale provides hope for all of us who feel like we've messed up, and our lives are beyond repair. Consequences for our sins certainly come, but God is willing and able to change your story in a moment. All you must do is cry out to him in dependence, admitting your need for redemption, and you too can be saved. This hope applies to all people. Even though the spotlight of the Old Testament falls on the nation of Israel, the story of Ruth proves that the love of God knows no geographical or political boundaries. His loving care extends to all people, even outsiders like Ruth.

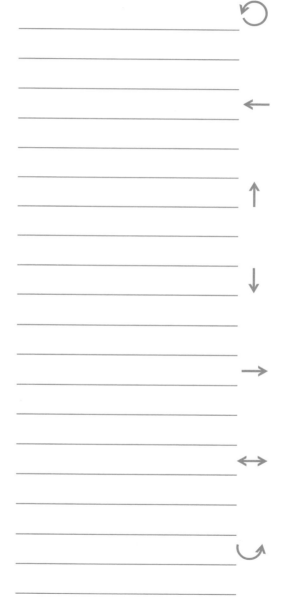

MATTHEW 1:1-6

↺ _____
_____
← _____
_____
_____
↑ _____
_____
_____
↓ _____
_____
_____
→ _____
_____
_____
↔ _____
_____
_____
↪ _____
_____
_____

Matthew began the story of Jesus' birth in a way most modern readers would consider strange. He began with Abraham and traced Jesus' genealogy. This should not seem as out of place to you now that you're beginning to understand the main theme of the Bible. Matthew showed the path God took to bring about the birth of the child who would fulfill the promises made to Adam and Eve so long ago. This child would be the serpent-crusher, who would destroy sin forever and rid the earth of sin's contamination. Just as promised, this child came to the earth through the line of Abraham and from the tribe of Judah. What's amazing to notice is some of the other people who make the list. In the first few verses are two names you now know: Boaz and Ruth. It turns out that the story in the book of Ruth isn't just a love story, it is God fulfilling His promise to send a child who would redeem in a far greater way than Boaz. Through faith in Christ, all people can find the redemption they so desperately need.

CHAPTER 5//KINGDOM

The fifth chapter in God's story describes the development of Israel into a powerful nation under the reign of three kings: Saul, David, and Solomon. The flow of God's story to this point has generally followed a chronological order—what happens in Exodus comes after what was recorded in Genesis, and so on. When we get to the kingdom chapter, the stories become a bit more difficult to follow. Various books record aspects of the development of the kingdom, at times telling the same stories with differing emphases. What's most important isn't that you know the names of each king or can plot the exact chronology of each of the stories. The primary theme you should notice is the failure of any human leader to provide a way for Israel to break free of their continual pattern of sinful rebellion.

The development of the kingdom was promised back in Genesis 12 when God pledged to grow Abram and his descendants into a great nation that would be a blessing to the whole world. It was never God's goal to simply love one nation at the expense of all the other people in the world. He chose Israel to be a unique reflection of His character. They experienced the salvation of God, received His law, and worshiped Him in His temple. The surrounding nations were meant to see a people who had been transformed by God's grace and be drawn to worship the one true God. The sin of the people caused them to miss out on their God-given mission and ultimately caused the nation to collapse.

As you read the stories of the men and women who lived and led during the kingdom of Israel, you'll likely see a lot that reminds you of yourself. There are stories of great faithfulness—stories where people trusted God and experienced His blessing. But these stories are often followed by stories of stunning failure—times when people made foolish choices that led to disastrous consequences.

You'll also observe the two dominant themes of the character of God. On one hand, you'll see examples of His holy judgment. He simply could not allow His people to mock His name through their ongoing disobedience—He punished sin, because blatant rebellion and God's holiness could not coexist. On the other hand, He demonstrated His persistent grace. Though the people proved incapable of obedience, He never gave up on His promises and refused to abandon His people. The answer to their sin would never come from a human king, as you'll soon see. Rather, God laid the groundwork for a far greater King who would establish an eternal kingdom.

1 SAMUEL 3

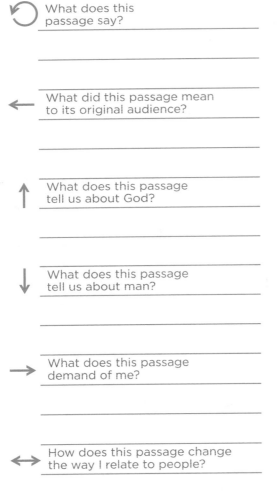

What does this
passage say?

What did this passage mean
to its original audience?

What does this passage
tell us about God?

What does this passage
tell us about man?

What does this passage
demand of me?

How does this passage change
the way I relate to people?

What does this passage
prompt me to pray to God?

Samuel appeared on the scene as a prophet sent by God to declare His Word to the nation of Israel during these dark days. Undoubtedly, Samuel had been set apart by God from birth to play this role. Samuel's message to the people was far from encouraging. In fact, through Samuel, God declared that He would punish the nation for their ongoing rebellion. Imagine what it must have been like to speak these words to the people—not the type of conversation likely to make many friends! But Samuel faithfully delivered God's message saying everything the Lord told him, even when that involved foretelling harm for the people. Samuel played a unique role, yet his work mirrors the task of all God's people today. We are to speak on behalf of God, warning others of the danger of their sin and begging them to turn to God for their salvation.

1 SAMUEL 4:1-10

The story told in chapter 4 symbolizes just how far the people of God had fallen. The ark of God—the tangible representation of His presence with the people and the house for the stone tablets on which were written God's law—was stolen by one of the foreign nations living in the land. In a bit of foreshadowing, God's presence was removed from His people and cast out among the nations, as God's people would soon be cast out of the land because of their sin. This was certainly bad news for God's people, but their story would become worse. Without God's presence leading the Israelites, the Philistines slaughtered them in battle. God had graciously revealed Himself to His people and lived in their midst, but He wanted the people to see and experience what happened when they tried to live without Him. Like Israel, we are inviting our own destruction when we ignore God and go through life on our own.

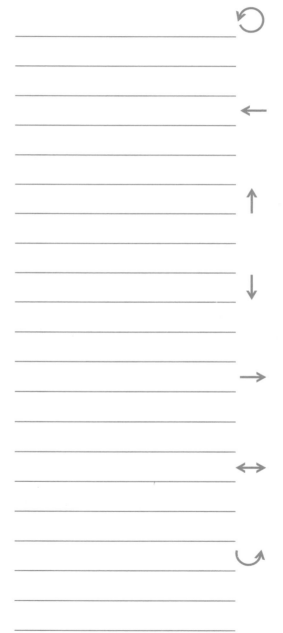

1 SAMUEL 5

↻ _____
_____
_____

← _____
_____
_____

↑ _____
_____
_____

↓ _____
_____
_____

→ _____
_____
_____

↔ _____
_____
_____

↰ _____
_____
_____

Even with the ark in captivity, God demonstrated His superiority over the so-called gods of the nations. One such false god, Dagon, was represented by a statue. When the ark entered Dagon's house, the false god literally crumbled in the presence of the glory of the one true God. They sent the ark on to another city where, after entering, the people were afflicted with tumors. Everywhere God's presence went, His power followed. And when His power invaded a place, especially a site of false worship, the greatness of God's glory caused every other thing to pale in comparison. God wants all people to learn this lesson: He is always greater than any false god, whatever that god might be— whether money, relationships, sports, popularity, power, education, or any other thing God created. Time and again, God will teach us that He is more important, more powerful, and more glorious than anything we might choose to worship in His place.

1 SAMUEL 8

Another consequence of the ongoing presence of the foreign nations in the promised land was God's people being drawn to their practices—not only their worship of false gods, but also the way they governed their people. The Israelites observed that all the other nations were led by kings. Israel was not. They assumed that if only a king ruled over them, like the other nations, then surely they would prevail over their enemies and have peace. But the absence of a king was intentional. God wanted the people to see Him as their King. He had already told Israel the path to victory and peace was found in listening to Him and following His Word, and not in electing a king. The people insisted on a king, and though Samuel warned them that this was a bad idea, they followed their own human wisdom and, once again, rebelled against God's plan.

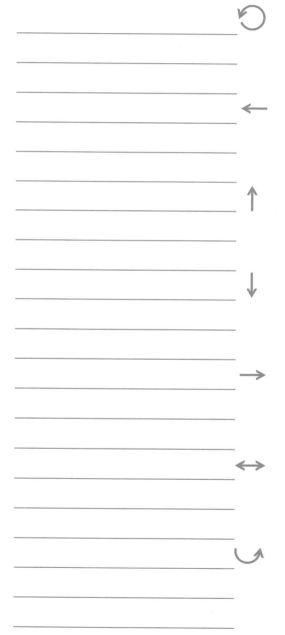

MATTHEW 27:27-31

⟲ _____

_____

← _____

_____

↑ _____

_____

↓ _____

_____

→ _____

_____

↔ _____

_____

↪ _____

_____

_____

Jesus' death may seem to be the final victory for Satan. Though Jesus was without sin, the Jewish leaders executed Him, and the wrath of God for people's sin was poured out on Jesus. The irony is not lost on the biblical writers—Jesus was dressed in kingly robes, given a crown of thorns, and called the King of the Jews. Certainly the authorities meant each of these acts as mockery, but they did not know that they were actually communicating a deep truth, one that the Israelites failed to understand. Jesus was, in fact, the King of the Jews. He came to do what no human leader in the Old Testament could do. The people asked for a king and they got fallen sinners as leaders. All along, God wanted to lead them, and through Jesus, God leads His people as the one true King.

1 SAMUEL 10:17-27

Saul was chosen as the first king in Israel. The method by which he was selected might seem a bit strange. The people did not vote for a certain king. Instead they cast lots, an ancient method of seeking to discover God's appointed leader. The chosen one was anointed with oil, intended to represent God's appointment of the leader. Saul was appointed to kingship, but it was clear that His appointment was more a curse than a blessing, as the lot fell to a man who was of the tribe of Benjamin. Samuel warned the people of the consequences of their choice—remember, way back in Genesis 49, God said that His chosen leader would come from the tribe of Judah, not Benjamin. God used the people's request for a king to bring judgment on the nation, rather than blessing through the godly leader they needed. As will soon become clear, the consequences of Saul's appointment as king would ultimately unravel the nation.

What does this passage say?

What did this passage mean to its original audience?

What does this passage tell us about God?

What does this passage tell us about man?

What does this passage demand of me?

How does this passage change the way I relate to people?

What does this passage prompt me to pray to God?

1 SAMUEL 15:10-35

↺ _____
_____
← _____
_____
_____
↑ _____
_____
_____
↓ _____
_____
_____
→ _____
_____
_____
↔ _____
_____
_____
↰ _____
_____
_____

Rather than leading Israel to make better decisions and follow God's plan, Saul continued the practices that landed them in trouble in the first place. The goal of Israel at this time was to drive out the foreign inhabitants of the promised land and to destroy the worship of false gods. Instead, the people plundered the goods of those they defeated in battle and took what they wanted for themselves. Some even went so far as to offer sacrifices to God from the spoils they claimed in victory. God, through the prophet Samuel, reminded the people that He did not need their sacrifices. He wanted their obedience. Because Saul embraced these foolish practices and led the people in rebellion, God removed Saul as king. Saul will continue to show up throughout the coming books of the Bible, but his God-appointed leadership of the people was over. The question was simply who would emerge as the next king, and would he fare any better?

1 SAMUEL 16:1-13

We don't have to wait long to find out who God chose as the next king. Once again, Samuel declared God's intention to the people. David, the next king, was an unlikely choice. There were other men among the nation far more qualified and who had the appearance one would expect of a king. But God doesn't make decisions the way you and I often do. He doesn't choose based on outward appearances of power, stature, or strength. Rather, He looks at the heart. God demonstrated that He sees and knows all things by choosing David, a man whom He would later describe as having a heart that pleases God. We should be reminded through the story of David that God often uses the unlikely to accomplish His good purposes, and that it is far more important for our hearts to be right with Him than for us to possess unique wisdom or strength. We appear to please God on the outside, but if our hearts don't love and worship Him, then He isn't truly pleased.

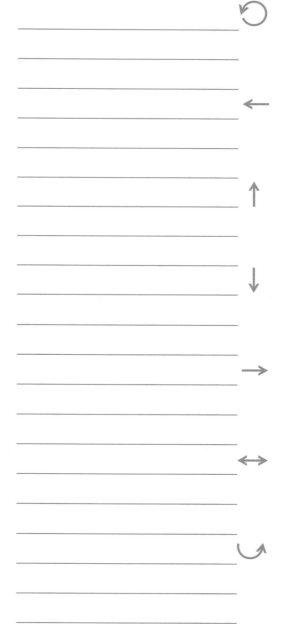

1 SAMUEL 17

↺ _____

_____

_____

← _____

_____

_____

↑ _____

_____

_____

↓ _____

_____

_____

→ _____

_____

_____

↔ _____

_____

_____

↪ _____

_____

_____

Though David had been chosen as the next king, He didn't immediately begin ruling the people. Instead, he watched sheep as a lowly shepherd out in the fields while his people, the Israelites, once again faced an imposing foe. Goliath—a Philistine and a massive mountain of a man taunted Israel and mocked their God. Everyone shook in their sandals, and no one would fight Goliath because of his imposing size. Like the Israelites on the brink of the promised land, God's people made decisions based on what their eyes saw instead of what God promised. David, on the other hand, trusted in the Lord and walked straight into battle with only a few stones. David's victory over Goliath proved, once again, that it was God who fought on behalf of His people. Those who walk by faith, regardless of their size or strength, will find that God always emerges victorious.

MARK 10:46-52

The story of the blind man named Bartimaeus recounts one of many stories where Jesus miraculously healed an individual. Sometimes He healed the blind or lame, and at times He even brought people back from death. These miracles paint a picture of what Jesus came to do. In a sin-infested world, people are born blind and lame, many experience various forms of sickness, and all people die. But Jesus came to change all this. One day, all forms of human brokenness will be no more. All those who know God will receive new bodies—resurrected bodies—that will be whole and healthy. The method Jesus used to heal demonstrated that all people could be eternally healed. Jesus brought healing based on the faith of others. Blind Bartimaeus knew He needed Jesus and had faith that Jesus could heal. Like David in the face of Goliath, Bartimaeus trusted in God as the only One who could overcome any enemy, even sickness and death. In the same way, all men and women can know eternal healing through faith in Jesus.

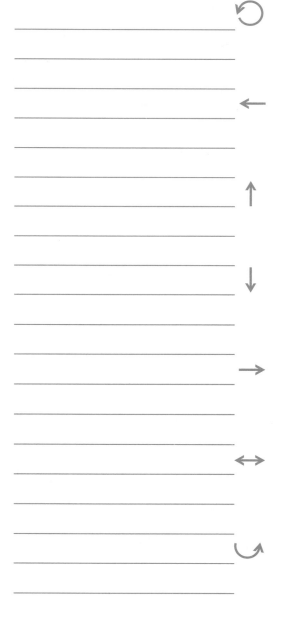

1 SAMUEL 18:6-16

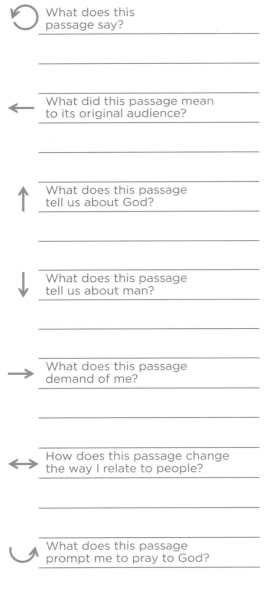

What does this passage say?

What did this passage mean to its original audience?

What does this passage tell us about God?

What does this passage tell us about man?

What does this passage demand of me?

How does this passage change the way I relate to people?

What does this passage prompt me to pray to God?

Saul no longer carried the title of God's chosen king, but he still craved power, and when David received praise for defeating Goliath, Saul exploded in anger. This jealousy sparked a rivalry Saul felt toward David for years to come. Saul and his men would seek to kill David time and again. When you read the psalms written by David, you will notice he often speaks of enemies like Saul seeking to destroy him. Throughout His life, David suffered at the hands of the first king of Israel. David certainly had enough trouble on his hands in the form of the foreign armies, but he also suffered from internal rivalries and division. The people of God quite literally imploded from the inside out. This tragic story reminds us of the great need for God's people to walk faithfully with God and live in unity with one another. Jealousy and division result from a sinful heart in rebellion to God, which can destroy people, churches, and even nations.

1 SAMUEL 24

David revealed his character by refusing to kill Saul. After David's victory over Goliath, Saul lived in pursuit of his archenemy. At this point, David had Saul trapped and had every reason to kill him on the spot. If he did, he would no longer have to fear Saul's jealous rage and live on the run. David resisted the temptation and spared Saul's life, leaving others in awe of such a godly choice. David understood that God did not delight in His people acting in anger and destroying others. Years later, Jesus would remind His followers that His people were to love their enemies, even praying for those who do them harm. This type of love flows only from God's Spirit working in the hearts of His children, causing them to respond as David did. Jesus is the perfect model of such love. After all, He gave His life as a sacrifice for His enemies.

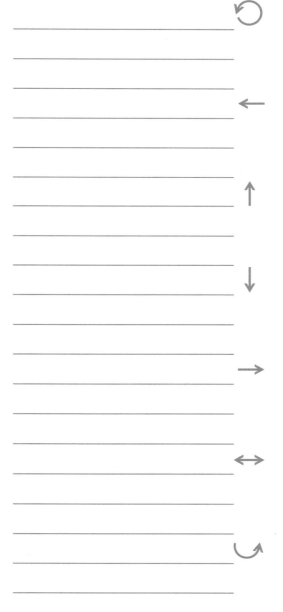

2 SAMUEL 5:1-10

↻ _____

_____

_____

← _____

_____

_____

↑ _____

_____

_____

↓ _____

_____

_____

→ _____

_____

_____

↔ _____

_____

_____

↱ _____

_____

_____

Saul's death began a series of battles over who would be king. Though David's anointing as king has already occurred, Saul's sons and followers still wanted to be his successors. However, God had already removed Saul's rule, so all the schemes of his descendants would come to nothing. Over and over, they were met with failure, while God's appointed leader continued to grow in might and power. The young shepherd boy who once protected and cared for flocks of sheep was established by God as the kingly shepherd leading the entire nation. A defining mark of David's rule would be the construction of a city which contained a temple for the worship of God. Soon the people would have what they'd been promised long ago—a good land on which to live, numerous descendants to proclaim God's glory, and a place where they could offer sacrifices for the forgiveness of their sins. It seems the time had finally come. Maybe David is the promised child who would defeat Satan, sin, and death?

1 CHRONICLES 15:25-29

We've moved forward a few books to Chronicles, which retells many of the stories found in 1 and 2 Samuel and 1 and 2 Kings. The primary purpose of Chronicles was to describe the genealogy of these key leaders, showing they fulfilled God's promise of a child from Abraham. Embedded in these genealogies are stories of the development and demise of Israel. The hope of the people of God was enhanced when the ark was brought back to the promised land—to Jerusalem. This was no small undertaking since the ark was a symbol of God's glory, presence, and holiness. A man named Uzzah merely touched the ark and died. It was clear that sinful humans could not approach God on their own. The people offered sacrifices as the ark traveled in hopes that they could move it back to its home without any further casualties. As they went, David danced before the Lord as an act of worship. He understood the significance of God's presence—without it, the people were doomed, but with God they could be victorious. He also understood that the proper response to God's glory was worship. Today, those who love God worship Him through singing, dancing, praying, and working—any action that shows the world that God is glorious.

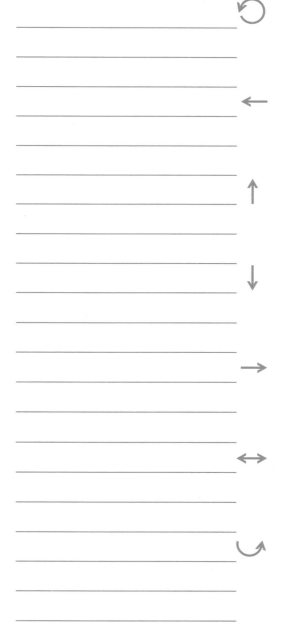

DAY 120

PSALM 95

The longest book in our Bibles, the book of Psalms, is a collection of songs and prayers from God's people during the time of the kings. Many of the psalms were written by King David in response to the circumstances of his life. Others were written by leaders of God's people as a reminder of God's faithfulness and the responsibility of the people to obey. Psalm 95 is one such example and encourages all of God's people to follow David's model of giving praise and worship to God. Music is one way that all people, throughout God's story, respond to His character and work in the world. These simple words of worship remind us of the various attributes of God revealed throughout His story—His love, kindness, grace, and mercy. The church today has the added benefit of knowing Jesus and understanding the fulfillment of God's promise through Him. Our reason for worship is clearer since Jesus appeared on the scene, and our worthy response should be praise for the glory of God revealed to us.

1 CHRONICLES 16:8-36

David's song recounted many of the important pieces of God's story that we have seen up to this point. He spent a lot of time praising God for His character. Glorious, holy, and powerful are just a few of the descriptions that David used to speak about God. But these qualities are not abstract—they've been concretely revealed in the way He dealt with the nation of Israel. By this point, there's no reason the nation should still exist. God could have wiped them out just like He did during the time of Noah. Instead, He continued to show steadfast love to His people. David claimed that God's love was based on the covenant He made with Israel long ago. He was the God of Abraham, Isaac, and Jacob, and He was at work fulfilling the promise He made to them. God's promises are more powerful than human sin. The same is true in your life. Salvation isn't based on your ability to be good, or else no one would be saved. Salvation is based on God's promise to save those who have faith in Jesus and nothing can take that salvation away.

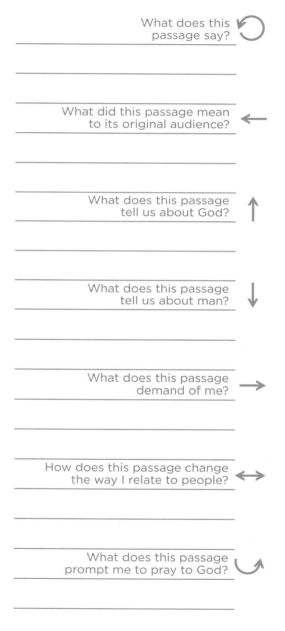

What does this passage say?

What did this passage mean to its original audience?

What does this passage tell us about God?

What does this passage tell us about man?

What does this passage demand of me?

How does this passage change the way I relate to people?

What does this passage prompt me to pray to God?

2 SAMUEL 7:1-17

God made another covenant with His people, this time declaring His promises to David. In this covenant, themes that we've seen before emerged. God pledged to bless David and his descendants and make them a great nation. This time, He used the language of kings to describe His promises. He pledged that David's throne would be established forever. Specifically, He pointed past David to his son, who would build a permanent house for the Lord in the promised land. From that lineage would also come the One who would fulfill the promise God made to Adam and Abraham. The description God gave here told us more about who this Child would be. He would be a king to lead God's people forever. In Genesis 49, we read that this child would come through the tribe of Judah, and the writer mentioned that He would carry a scepter, an object carried by a king. The blurry details are coming into greater focus the more we read God's story, but clearly God is doing exactly what He's always said He would do.

2 SAMUEL 9

The history books in our Bible, primarily 1 and 2 Samuel, 1 and 2 Kings, and 1 and 2 Chronicles, tell story after story of God's work through His people. These stories are filled with murder, romance, treachery, and even a bit of comedy thrown in the mix. The story told in 2 Samuel 9 was a heart-warming testimony to the character of David. In no way did Saul deserve David's kindness. In fact, Saul spent much of his life trying to kill David. How might you respond if someone treated you that way? You'd likely want revenge, or at the least you'd want that person out of your life forever. David did the exact opposite. Upon Saul's death, He pledged to care for his family as an act of honor to the former king and out of loyalty and friendship with Saul's son, Jonathan. Mephibosheth received King David's grace and, though he couldn't walk, David brought him to his table to eat meals. Mephibosheth represents all Christians, who have no right to be in God's presence, but receive grace to feast at the one, true King's table each and every day.

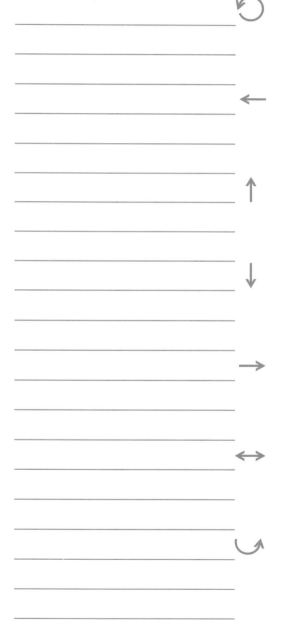

2 SAMUEL 11

↻ _____

_____

_____

← _____

_____

_____

↑ _____

_____

↓ _____

_____

_____

_____

→ _____

_____

_____

↔ _____

_____

_____

↰ _____

_____

_____

Following such a touching moment of kindness, David hit the lowest point of his life. David accomplished many great deeds, and he would do many more in the future. But here he messed up big time! We're left to guess at the motives behind David's actions. Maybe he was just caught in a moment of laziness and gave in to his human desires. Maybe he had been thinking about committing this act for some time. Maybe he let the power of being king get to his head and thought that he could get away with whatever he wanted. The sin that infested his heart came to the surface in a series of tragic choices. These were not mere mistakes—they were downright evil, and only David was to blame. The story of his sinful encounter with Bathsheba and the murder of her husband reminds us that all people are capable of great evil. We must consistently be on guard against Satan's attacks and never think that we are above making foolish decisions that could change our lives forever.

PSALM 51

David wrote Psalm 51 after he was caught in his sin with Bathsheba. David's reflections in this Psalm presented a beautiful picture for how all people should respond to their sin. David admitted that his sin was first and foremost against God. He broke God's law and therefore deserved any punishment given by a holy God. He also begged God to cleanse his sinful heart because he knew that God was the only one capable of forgiving sin. Finally, he asked God to replace his sorrow with joy and renew a deep love for God and the salvation He'd received. We should follow David's pattern when we sin as well. Rather than running and hiding with our sin, we should admit our evil to God and ask Him to cleanse us. We, who live after Jesus' death and resurrection, know far more about how God forgives sins than David could understand. We can confess our sin knowing sin's punishment has been satisfied through Jesus' death on the cross. While we should feel sorrow over our mistakes, our sin does not define us. We can walk in joy and freedom knowing God forgives.

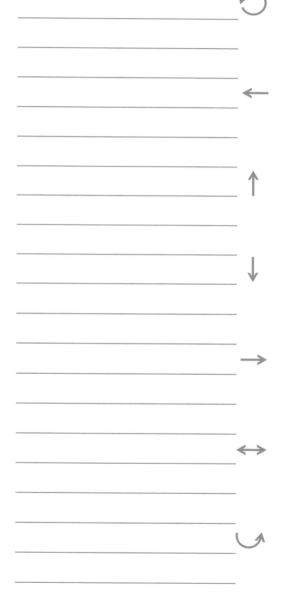

2 SAMUEL 15:1-6

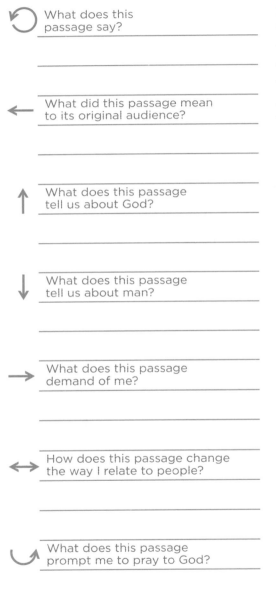

What does this passage say?

_____

_____

What did this passage mean to its original audience?

_____

_____

What does this passage tell us about God?

_____

_____

What does this passage tell us about man?

_____

_____

What does this passage demand of me?

_____

_____

How does this passage change the way I relate to people?

_____

_____

What does this passage prompt me to pray to God?

_____

_____

David's own son, Absalom, attempted to wrestle the kingship away from his father. He began a systematic process of convincing many Israelites that he would be a far better king, and that they should follow him. Many did. The result was a series of stories in which the people chose sides between Absalom and David. The fracturing of the nation of Israel had begun. God knew this would be the outcome when He warned the people against appointing a human king. Power corrupts and, in the hands of sinful people, there would be no end to the fighting between various leaders who wanted to rule. It was clear that God was the one who actually appointed kings, yet we're told that Absalom was handsome and highly praised. People follow men like that, regardless of whether God has chosen them. We're reminded through the story of Absalom that we must be careful who we follow because some leaders will cause us great harm.

PSALM 3

Most of us would not think to write songs when hiding from an enemy who wanted us dead—much less sing them. David wrote Psalm 3 while running from his son, who wanted David ousted as king, so that he could take the throne. Foremost in David's mind was the fact that the infighting made God look bad. People knew that God had anointed David as king. Look at David now—on the run and hiding. David crafted this Psalm to remind himself that God had not abandoned him, even though it might look like it to outsiders. God remained by David's side, fighting on his behalf and protecting his life. All Christians face this type of challenge. When we trust Jesus, our lives aren't automatically free of pain. We still suffer, and in moments of pain, we have to remind ourselves that God is for us. When people look at our lives and question why God would let bad things happen to us, we must remind ourselves that God is at work in thousands of ways we cannot see, and we can always trust Him.

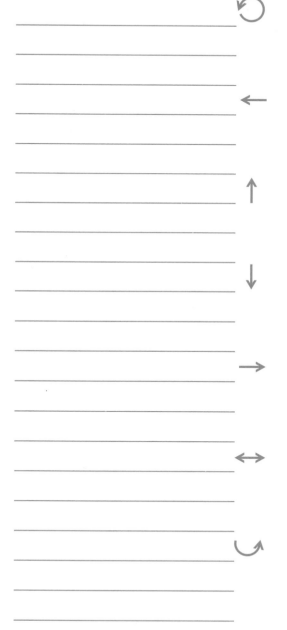

1 CHRONICLES 22:6-19

↻ _____
_____
← _____
_____
↑ _____
_____
↓ _____
_____
→ _____
_____
↔ _____
_____
↪ _____
_____
_____

The task of building a permanent dwelling place for God rested on David's son, Solomon, and this work had been a long time coming. In the wilderness, the Israelites constructed a makeshift tent, known as the tabernacle, to house the ark of the covenant. Now in the promised land, it was time to get to work building a grand temple. Though they did not deserve it, God gave Israel rest from constant warfare in order to allow them time to complete this work. The temple was not merely the place where Israelites would worship God through the offering of sacrifices. God told Solomon the temple would be the house for His name, a picture of His glory. The sheer size and splendor of the temple was to be a picture of the greatness of God. The temple would be a constant reminder of how blessed the Israelites were—they had a personal relationship with God. The surrounding nations would know that Israel's God was far different from the false gods that they worshiped.

1 KINGS 3:3-15

Solomon, like his father David, was a complicated figure. He loved God and walked in obedience to Him— he sought to keep God's Word and lead others to do the same. But he also continued to offer sacrifices at the places where the surrounding nations worshiped false gods. Once again, God willingly worked through a broken person to continue His mission in the world. Solomon seemed to understand the weight of his task because, when given the opportunity to ask the Lord for anything, he requested wisdom. Imagine that you were Solomon—you might be tempted to ask for power, wealth, or health. Solomon chose wisdom, and he received power, wealth, and health to go along with it. This wisdom allowed Solomon to lead a nation which was on the brink of destruction due to their sin. Solomon's wisdom was a gift of God, not something he gained or earned on his own. Though he possessed unrivaled power, fame, and wisdom, God intended for Solomon to use these gifts to reflect God's image in the world.

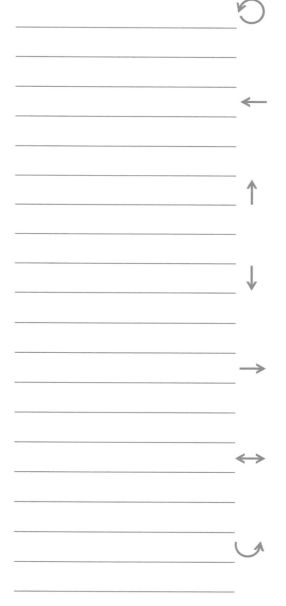

1 CORINTHIANS 2:6-16

↺ _____

_____

_____

← _____

_____

_____

↑ _____

_____

_____

↓ _____

_____

_____

→ _____

_____

_____

↔ _____

_____

_____

↪ _____

_____

_____

God is the foundation of all wisdom. As the Creator of all that exists, He literally knows everything about everything! Sinful humans lack such wisdom, and in fact, our best efforts at understanding ourselves and our world are doomed from the start. Our sin makes it impossible for us to comprehend the wisdom of God. That's why God's Spirit is vital, according to Paul. The Spirit of God knows the mind of God and reveals it to the children of God. When a person becomes a Christian, the Spirit of God fills that person's life, much as the glory of God filled the temple in the Old Testament. Filled with God's Spirit, we are able to find insight and wisdom that would be impossible on our own. The most important aspect of this wisdom comes as the Spirit gives us understanding regarding God's mission in the world. This is a story none of us could dream up or invent on our own. It's a story only God could write, and He graciously reveals it to us. Without the Spirit of God revealing His plan, we would never grasp it, much less respond in faith. The Spirit continues revealing God's character and His work in our lives as we listen and follow Him each day.

1 KINGS 4:20-34

We observe God's love for His people in the way He used so many men and women in the Old Testament to write down His wisdom for future generations. Some of these individuals served to teach us through their example—both positive and negative. Others pointed us to God through their writing. David, Solomon, and Paul were uniquely gifted by God to preserve His Word for future generations. The book of Proverbs is a collection of the wisdom God gave Solomon, who then wrote it down as instruction for his son. The practical wisdom found in Proverbs demonstrates the way God's wisdom should shape our speech, finances, relationships, and other everyday choices we face. Over and over, Solomon reminded his readers that true wisdom could only be found by knowing the Lord and humbly submitting to His ways. In a world filled with voices telling us how we should live, it's necessary that we look to the wisdom that comes from God. Others might give us good pointers on life, but only God knows true wisdom.

What does this passage say?

What did this passage mean to its original audience?

What does this passage tell us about God?

What does this passage tell us about man?

What does this passage demand of me?

How does this passage change the way I relate to people?

What does this passage prompt me to pray to God?

PROVERBS 1:1-7

↺ _____
_____
_____
← _____
_____
↑ _____
_____
↓ _____
_____
→ _____
_____
_____
↔ _____
_____
_____
↪ _____
_____
_____

The book of Proverbs begins with the main point of the entire book. Those who are considered wise in this world are actually fools if they do not know God. The truly wise individual are the one who fear the Lord. Fear should arise as a normal response to God—after all, His glory is overwhelming! That's likely why so many people fell down on their faces in worship when they met Jesus, or why God could not let Moses see Him without a veil over his face. The amazing holiness of God and His great power makes us helpless, so all we can do is stand in awe. We should tremble because we know that we are not holy. God has every right to pour out His wrath on us for our sin. This is what makes the gospel extraordinary—the same God who causes us to tremble, invites us to call Him Father. The God who could condemn us in judgment, invites us lovingly into His presence. The God who knows all things reminds us that He will graciously guide us to all wisdom if we simply ask.

1 KINGS 6

God took great care in the construction of His temple. No detail was too small or beyond His notice. He shaped the temple to reflect His holiness and made it possible for sinful humans to worship Him. Of particular note are the cherubim, or angels, that filled the temple. If you remember back in Genesis 3, God kicked Adam and Eve out of the garden due to their sin. They once were able to walk and talk with God in the garden as a man does with his friend, but they were forever banished from His presence. Afterward, God stationed angels around the garden of Eden, so that Adam and Eve and their descendants could never reenter the garden and His presence. Centuries later, the temple modeled the garden. It was a physical location where God lived among His people. The angels still guard God's presence, but God invites us into His presence, not cutting us off completely. But to enter His presence, a sacrifice is required. The picture is clear—a relationship with God is made possible by a sacrificial substitute. The only way you come to God is through faith in Jesus' sacrifice.

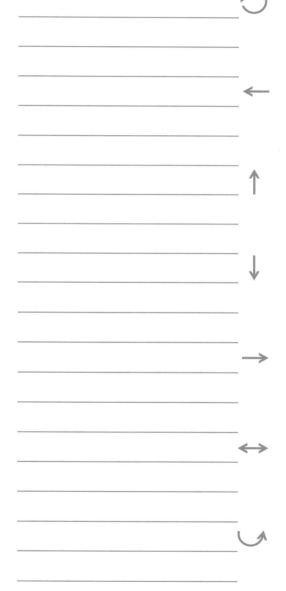

2 CHRONICLES 5:2-14

↻ _____
_____
_____
← _____
_____
_____
↑ _____
_____
_____
↓ _____
_____
_____
_____
→ _____
_____
_____
↔ _____
_____
_____
↺ _____
_____
_____

After years of wilderness wandering and still more years of fighting in the land, the temple was complete and, when the ark was brought inside, God filled the temple with His glorious presence. The sounds of singing, dancing, and praise filled the air. Altogether, the people proclaimed the big idea of the Old Testament—God is good and His steadfast love endures forever. They looked back over their nation's history and recognized they were stiff-necked, half-hearted, and sinful through and through. They were the unworthy recipients of God's blessings, but there they were before God's temple in a land they did not deserve. For those who have a personal relationship with God through faith in Jesus Christ, though we don't deserve God's blessings, we are blessed beyond measure. In spite of our sin, God loves us and lives in us. He is good and His steadfast love endures forever.

1 CORINTHIANS 6:12-20

Something unique happened after Jesus' death, resurrection, and ascension. In the Old Testament, God lived among His people in the tabernacle and later in the temple. These were physical structures built by man that God inhabited, filling them with His glory. Following Jesus, God's glory does not fill temples—it fills people. God's Spirit lives inside those who have placed their faith in Christ. That's why we can gather with other Christians in all different types of buildings as the church. The building isn't most important. What's important is that God's lives inside us! Paul made this point to the church in Corinth, a church engaged in all sorts of sinful behavior. He argued that the people should put away their sinful ways because their bodies were a temple of God. Everywhere we go, everything we do, is done in full view of God who lives inside us. There's no chance any of us can sin without God knowing because He knows all things and lives in us by His Spirit. This means everything we do is either an expression of worship to God or rebellion against Him.

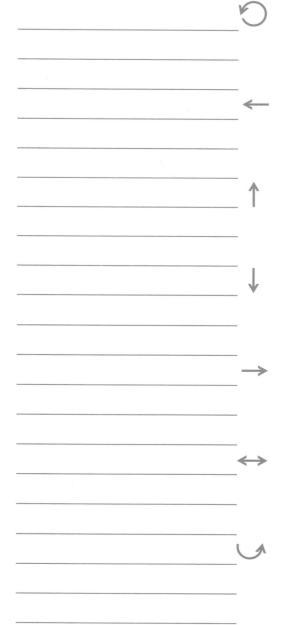

1 KINGS 9:1-9

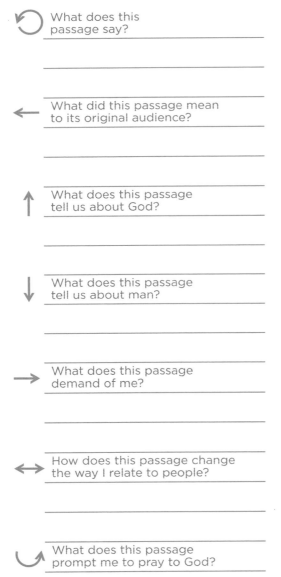

What does this
passage say?

What did this passage mean
to its original audience?

What does this passage
tell us about God?

What does this passage
tell us about man?

What does this passage
demand of me?

How does this passage change
the way I relate to people?

What does this passage
prompt me to pray to God?

It appears that God said two differing things here. First, God told Solomon that He was going to establish Solomon's kingdom forever. Then, he warned Solomon that if he failed to obey God, He would destroy the temple that Solomon had just finished. So which is it? Both! The first commitment was based solely on the character of God. He promised to establish David's kingly line through his son, Solomon, and God would keep that promise regardless of what Solomon or the people did. But that didn't mean that Solomon could do whatever he wanted. There are always consequences for actions. In this case, the consequence for Solomon and the people's disobedience would result in God destroying the temple and kicking them out of the promised land. The same truth applies to us today, though we don't have a promised land or a temple. God's love through Christ is based on His commitment to save His children. But we will still experience consequences when we choose to disobey God. In this life, actions will have consequences and God often uses the pain we experience to bring us to repentance.

1 KINGS 11:1-8

It didn't take long for Solomon to follow the path of his father, David, and of the nation of Israel. After taking many wives from among the nations, Solomon's heart was drawn to worship their gods as his own. The very same man whom God used to build His temple began building altars where he and others could worship false gods. This same story is, as you've seen, repeated over and over. First, it was the nation of Israel building a golden calf at the base of the mountain while Moses was meeting with God face-to-face. In Solomon, these two aspects of humanity—the good and the bad—were vividly portrayed in the same person. Two emotions should swell in our hearts. One is humility because we know that we are also sinful and broken. Even on our best days, we are capable of great evil. The second emotion is joy, because we know God loves us despite our patterns of sin. Just as God used Solomon in significant ways, God can use sinners like you and me to play a key role in His mission in the world.

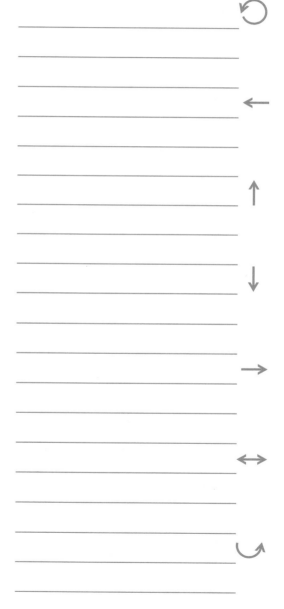

2 CHRONICLES 10

↺ _____

_____

← _____

_____

_____

↑ _____

_____

↓ _____

_____

_____

→ _____

_____

_____

↔ _____

_____

_____

↱ _____

_____

_____

After Solomon's death, the story of the kings of Israel followed tragically one after another. The Bible focused on three main kings—Saul, David, and Solomon. They played a unique role in God's mission in both good ways and bad. The details of the kings who followed are recorded in much less detail. In fact, their stories often amount to simple descriptions of when the king ruled and whether or not he was faithful to God during his rule. Along the way, however, there was a constant theme of unrest among God's people. Their stories didn't exactly read like what you would expect from a group of people who were now living in the promised land, having finally completed the construction of the temple. When Solomon died, immediately various factions began to campaign for the next king. Ten tribes refused to follow Solomon's son, Rehoboam, and united around Jeroboam instead. From this point forward, the nation was divided into two factions: Israel in the north and Judah in the south. God's people, the ones who had experienced His miraculous presence, turned against each other. Their demise was certain.

1 KINGS 17

Bad times became a reality for the people of God. Not only had they failed to drive out the inhabitants in the land, but they turned on themselves and the kingdom became divided. Two figures played a prominent role during this stage of God's story: Elijah and Elisha. Both men were called speak on God's behalf and warn the people of their coming destruction. Can you imagine how unpopular such a message made them? Their lives, however, testify to God's power in unique ways. They performed various miracles, proving they were from God and were demonstrating God's power to overcome the effects of sin and death. Elijah and Elisha confirmed that, even in the worst of times, God raises up individuals to speak and lead on His behalf. When everyone else falls away, there are those given the responsibility to call others to return to God. It takes great courage to speak up when others rebel against God, but those who do will experience God's power at work in their lives.

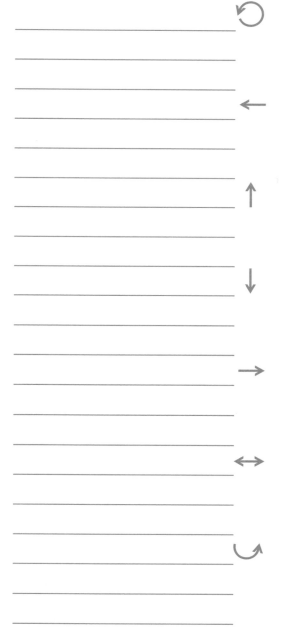

DAY 140

MATTHEW 17:1-13

↺ _____

← _____

↑ _____

↓ _____

→ _____

↔ _____

↩ _____

Jesus came to earth as 100 percent God, but also 100 percent man. There has never been, nor will there ever be, anyone like Him. During his earthly ministry, people saw and interacted with Jesus the man without fully understanding they were also standing face-to-face with God. Jesus constantly worked to reveal to others His true identity and purpose. At His baptism, a voice spoke from heaven declaring Jesus to be the Son of God. Later, near the end of His ministry, another scene from heaven revealed Jesus' unique identity. All that happened at the transfiguration wasn't exactly clear, but we did clearly see Peter, James, and John were given a special glimpse of the glory of God in the person of Jesus. Two prominent figures from the Old Testament—Moses and Elijah–appeared with Jesus, showing that Jesus' work was a continuation and fulfillment of the work these two men began. Moses and Elijah were great men used by God to lead Israel, but they were not God. Only Jesus is both God and man.

1 KINGS 18:1-40

Elijah was not the only prophet in his day. There were hundreds of other false prophets supposedly speaking on behalf of Baal, a false god whom the nations, as well as many within Israel, worshiped. Elijah first challenged the people's allegiance by reminding them that they could not continue to serve multiple gods. They had to decide whether they would worship the true and living God or these false gods. Before the people chose, God demonstrated that He was the supreme and only true God. With a contest between His prophet, Elijah, and the false prophets, God made it clear that false gods couldn't hear or answer. That's the problem with false gods—they never come through and they always let us down. God, however, always answers according to His will. He even stacks the odds against Himself to prove His power. Through stories like this, we should be reminded that idols will let us down as well. Relationships, sports, money, power, or any other created thing will never provide for our deepest needs. Only God can.

What does this passage say?

What did this passage mean to its original audience?

What does this passage tell us about God?

What does this passage tell us about man?

What does this passage demand of me?

How does this passage change the way I relate to people?

What does this passage prompt me to pray to God?

1 KINGS 19:9-18

↻ _____
_____
_____
← _____
_____
_____
↑ _____
_____
↓ _____
_____
_____
→ _____
_____
_____
↔ _____
_____
_____
_____
↪ _____
_____
_____

Elijah experienced a unique relationship with God. Like many of the key leaders in the Old Testament, Elijah had an intimate relationship with God. God spoke with Elijah and used Him to bring God's Word to the nation. After defeating the prophets of Baal, God spoke to Elijah again, this time in a way you might not expect. How do you think the voice that spoke creation into existence might sound? Maybe loud and commanding? At times, God does speak this way. But He spoke to Elijah in a quiet whisper. Elijah, because he faithfully listened to God and passionately protected the honor of God's name, heard God even in the silence. We've seen throughout the Old Testament that God continually revealed Himself to His people. If not for the self-revelation of God, we would have no hope of knowing Him. But God continually speaks to His people. In a world filled with noise, it's important to remember that we must be still and quiet in order to hear from God.

2 KINGS 2

You've got to love the curveballs the Bible throws! Chants at bald guys and attacking bears—who doesn't love that kind of action? Miracles of God filled the stories of Elijah and Elisha in the midst of the chaos of a sinful nation. Both men served as prophets of God, which means they listened to God's Word and spoke to the people. Often the message spoken through the prophets was negative, warning of the punishment to come because of the people's sin. The Bible tells the stories of these two, and also contains the writings of many other prophets who played a similar role—men like Isaiah, Jeremiah, Ezekiel, Micah, and others. The prophets' function parallels the task of Christians today. They were to use their voices and lives to declare God's Word and demonstrate His power. Either task isolated from the other was insufficient. They could not merely speak God's Word and live an unchanged life, nor could they demonstrate a godly life without speaking God's Word. These two tasks—speaking and living—mark those God uses in powerful ways.

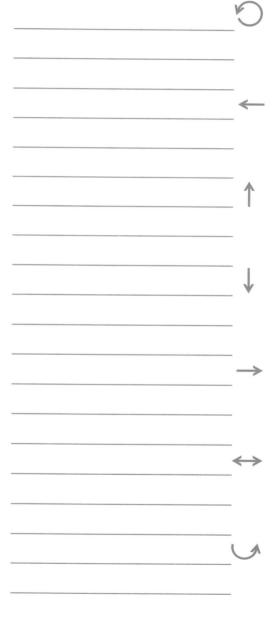

2 KINGS 5:1-14

↺ _____

_____

← _____

_____

↑ _____

_____

↓ _____

_____

_____

→ _____

_____

_____

↔ _____

_____

_____

↪ _____

_____

_____

Hidden among all the stories of the kings in Israel and Judah are stories like this, of an individual who experienced the power of God in a personal way. Throughout the Bible, leprosy served as a picture of sin. This brutal disease killed a person as, inch by inch, his flesh was eaten away. Not only was the disease excruciating, but those with leprosy were forbidden interaction with other people. Further, they lost the privilege of worshiping God in the temple. The leper was completely cut off. Naaman was not the type of person you'd expect God to heal since he was not an Israelite. But God proved there are no national limits concerning His healing power. God used His people—a little girl and the prophet Elisha—to bless Naaman and show Him the power of God. All Israel was meant to do this! They were called out to be a light to the nations and a reflection of God's glory. The nation's sin caused them to abandon this mission, but God continued to work through a few faithful ones, showing that He had not given up. All Naaman had to do was listen to God's Word and have faith in His plan, and he experienced healing from God.

1 JOHN 1:5-10

Sin makes people dirty. Like Naaman the leper, our sin is hideous, and what we need most in life is to be clean. This is why the Bible is full of scenes of people washing themselves before they come to worship. People had to be cleansed of their filth before they could worship a pure God. Still today, you can observe ceremonial washing stations beside mosques and temples in many parts of the world. Why don't we wash ourselves in this way when we come to church? The answer is found in 1 John 1. John said that cleansing came not by taking a bath, but through belief and confession. If we repent of our sins and have faith in Jesus' work, we can be cleansed of our spiritual leprosy. Baptism serves as a picture of this great truth—those who have faith in Jesus are immersed under the water and brought back out as a picture of the cleansing that has already come through their faith in Jesus. Those who have been cleaned by Jesus have no need to be washed again—they are forever clean!

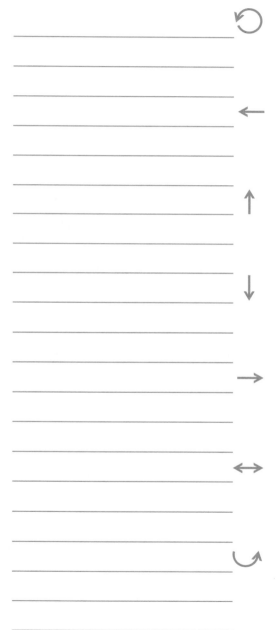

CHAPTER 6//JUDGMENT

The final chapter of God's story found in the Old Testament tells of God's judgment. We've already seen episodes of God's judgment throughout the Bible. Starting with Noah, God's wrath was poured out on the sin and brokenness of His world. Later, specific locations such as Sodom and Gomorrah received a similar punishment for their wrongdoing. God has proven that He will not look the other way pretending that sin doesn't exist. His holiness and character require judgment for sin.

Following every stage of judgment, there seems to be slight hope that God's people will change and finally live in obedience to Him. Such obedience is, over and over again, short-lived. Israel acts like a young child who's been disciplined for being mean to his sister. Once he's caught in sin he says he's sorry, only to be mean to her again as soon as he thinks his parents aren't looking. The good behavior that follows the punishment doesn't last.

God threatened a more widespread judgment for His people after crossing into the promised land. If they did not uphold their end of the covenant they had made with God, they would be kicked off the land. If they continued to worship the false gods of the surrounding nations and rebel against the one true God, they would suffer the consequences.

The fifth chapter of God's story reveals the main problem with humans—they continue to sin even though they know they are doing wrong. Have you noticed this in your own life? The Bible often describes sin as slavery, because that's the way it works in our lives. It traps us. We're caught, and even when we want to escape, we simply can't get out on our own.

Our problem is the same as the nation of Israel. It's not just that we occasionally do bad things. The problem stems from hearts that desire to rebel against God, and we're totally incapable of changing our hearts. If the answer was found in trying to be better, we'd have no hope. God gave a much different answer. As we will see throughout this chapter of judgment, He promised to send someone who would do something about the sin of the human heart. After judgment comes salvation—this time it will be a salvation that will last.

ISAIAH 1

God consistently warned His people of their impending doom. The era of the kings had been an overwhelming failure, and things were moving from bad to worse. Along the way, God raised up prophets who spoke to the people reminding them of their covenant commitment to God. Our Bible contains the writings of five major prophets and twelve minor prophets. When you read the words "major" and "minor," don't assume that the major prophets are more important. The distinction is simply based on the length of the books. There's much debate as to the exact time when each of the prophets spoke to the people, but we can divide them into three main groups: (1) those who wrote before Israel was kicked out of the promised land, (2) those who wrote while the nations were living as exiles outside of the land, and (3) those who wrote after some Israelites were allowed to return to the land. One of the most prominent prophets to warn the nation before they were judged was Isaiah. His opening chapter, addressed to the southern tribes in Judah, demonstrated the enormity of God's anger over the sin of the people. Though the chapter hints at the offer of forgiveness, it is clear that God is about to judge severely.

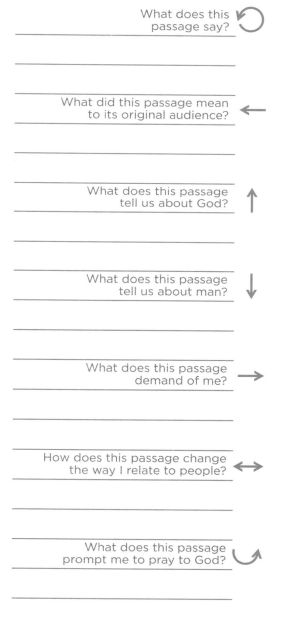

What does this passage say?

What did this passage mean to its original audience?

What does this passage tell us about God?

What does this passage tell us about man?

What does this passage demand of me?

How does this passage change the way I relate to people?

What does this passage prompt me to pray to God?

JEREMIAH 2:4-13

↻ _____
_____
_____
← _____
_____
_____
↑ _____
_____
_____
↓ _____
_____
_____
→ _____
_____
_____
↔ _____
_____
_____
↱ _____
_____
_____

God accused His people of two sins. First, they abandoned God. This choice was stunning because, as Jeremiah reminded the people, God had been faithful to them, leading them since their time of slavery in Egypt. Second, and equally disastrous, they had created their own gods to worship. Jeremiah, speaking on behalf of God, compared this to a cistern, a reservoir in the ground that held water. The nation chose to abandon the cistern that provided healthy water, instead choosing to dig their own cisterns that couldn't even hold water, much less provide water to meet their needs. The coming judgment was their own fault, a reality God pointed out time and again through prophets like Jeremiah, both here and in the book of Lamentations. The downfall of Israel reminds us that sin always has consequences, and we have no one to blame but ourselves.

JEREMIAH 31:31-34

The prophet Jeremiah used the familiar word "covenant" to describe the way God would deal with His people. Prophets like Jeremiah often spoke of the future in varying stages. At times, the prophets described the immediate future. The book of Jeremiah referred to the time when the nation would be judged for their sin and removed from the land. Other times, they spoke of the distant future—when the fulfillment of God's promises through Jesus would come to pass. Still other times, they described the final judgment when Jesus will return and declare His final victory. Here Jeremiah spoke of the second stage. After God's first judgment, He would fulfill His covenant by forgiving the sins of His people and by giving them a new heart capable of loving God and others as they were created to do in the first place.

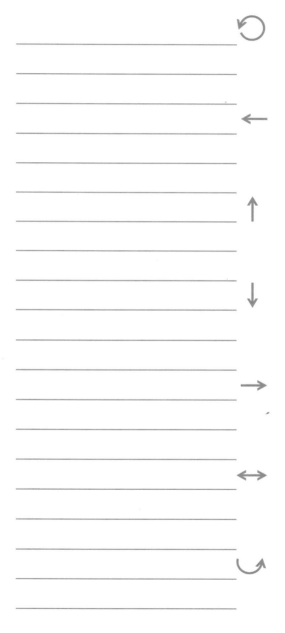

DAY 149

JEREMIAH 32:36-44

God often spoke of His personal relationship to Israel with this language—"They will be my people, and I will be their God." It's amazing to consider the grace of God in allowing an entire nation of sinful people to claim God as their God. He went even further and said that He would find great joy in doing good to His people after they experienced the consequences for their sin. This revealed God's deep love for His people. His love is altogether different than the love we express to one another. It's uncommon for someone to find joy in doing good to someone who has done them great harm, but this is the kind of love God shows us through Jesus. He died for us while we were still sinners and did not wait for us to become lovable. He simply delights in showing love to sinners.

ISAIAH 53

Not all that the prophets said or wrote was bad news. Remember, the future promises of God are still in effect. He would still defeat Satan, sin, and death through a child of Eve, the line of Abraham, the tribe of Judah, and the throne of David. No amount of human sin could stop this from happening. Isaiah 53 is filled with the good news of this coming One, though the images used are not what most would expect from the coming Savior. We're given one of the most vivid pictures of the crucifixion of Jesus found in the Old Testament. The Savior would be crushed for human sin, and like a sacrificial lamb, slaughtered so that we might live. Even more striking, we're told that this is God's will—it was God's plan all along to kill this One so that sinners could be forgiven.

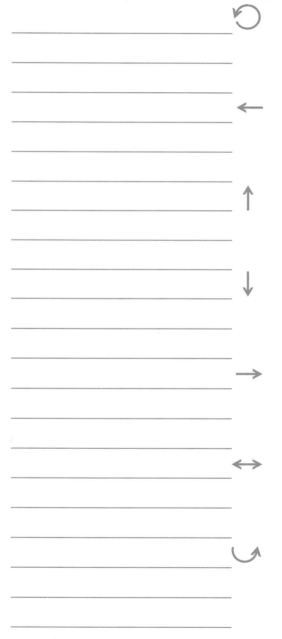

MICAH 5

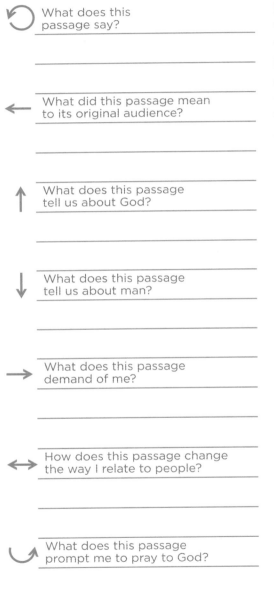

What does this passage say?

_____

_____

_____

What did this passage mean to its original audience?

_____

_____

_____

What does this passage tell us about God?

_____

_____

_____

What does this passage tell us about man?

_____

_____

_____

What does this passage demand of me?

_____

_____

_____

How does this passage change the way I relate to people?

_____

_____

_____

What does this passage prompt me to pray to God?

_____

_____

_____

Micah is one of several minor prophets who spoke to God's people before they were sent into exile. Each book has a very similar theme—God's people sinned, they deserved judgment, and God would carry it out. The warnings were intense and severe. The prophets also contain some of the most beautiful images of the fulfillment of God's promise to save sinners and fix this broken world. Hundreds of years before Jesus' birth, the prophet Micah connected this coming One to God's promises from long ago—He would be from the clan of Judah and a ruler like David. Micah also pointed forward to the fact that this One would come from Bethlehem. Centuries later, a baby lying in a manger fulfilled this prophecy. One of the primary ways we know the truthfulness and trustworthiness of the Bible is how specific it is about details in history that actually happened.

AMOS 3

The majority of books like Amos, Obadiah, and Zephaniah consists of warnings about the coming judgment and inviting the people to turn back to God. They reminded God's people that, although the warnings about judgment were dire, they had not yet come to pass. If Israel or Judah would repent and commit themselves once again to obeying God with all their hearts, the coming judgment could be avoided. Though the people had a track record of failure, God was still willing to forgive should they change. Amos accused the people of not listening. They were like a kid with his fingers in his ears so he wouldn't hear his mom telling him to do his chores. They could hear, but they refused to listen. It's not as if God was unjust in His judgment or too swift in His wrath. He gave them every opportunity to repent and be saved. Sadly, we often do the very same thing. We know the good we should be doing, but we fail to listen to God and to those who seek to point us to His Word.

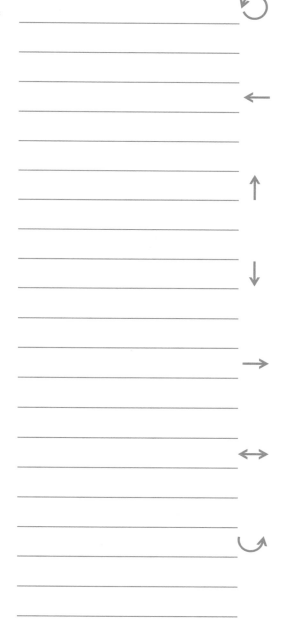

JONAH 1

The book of Jonah is a familiar story to many. God called Jonah, one of His prophets, to go to Nineveh and speak to them about God's coming judgment. Jonah did the exact opposite and chose to flee from God's plan. We find out later one of the main reasons Jonah didn't go to Nineveh—he feared that the people of this pagan city would repent and turn to God. Jonah wanted God to wipe them out and not accept them after their repentance. Jonah's fears came true. After God altered Jonah's path with the help of a big fish, Jonah delivered the word of God to the people, many repented, and God relented from destroying the city. However, their change of heart was short-lived. Soon after the prophet Nahum would once again speak concerning the coming destruction of Nineveh. God's patience in judgment shows us that He longs to see people turn to Him and be saved. He'll wait and wait, not desiring any to perish but that all would be saved. Every day you live is another day God graciously gives you to turn to Him and be saved from His wrath.

HABAKKUK 3:17-19

Destruction was looming on the horizon for Israel. They had witnessed God's power when He judged others for sin, and Israel themselves had experienced the consequences for their sin in the past. But what they would experience in the days ahead was unlike anything they'd seen to this point. The prophet Habakkuk looked toward the awaiting devastation and spoke truth that is critical for all people to understand when experiencing pain and suffering. Habakkuk understood that the most important aspect of life wasn't momentary fulfillment—it wasn't food, clothing, or anything this life had to offer. What's most important is the salvation of God. Even when all of life seemed to spiral out of control, Habakkuk found joy in God and His salvation. Prophets like Joel reminded the nation that, in the days ahead, God would restore the fortunes of His people. For the time however, even in pain, Habakkuk could find joy simply in knowing God and experiencing His love.

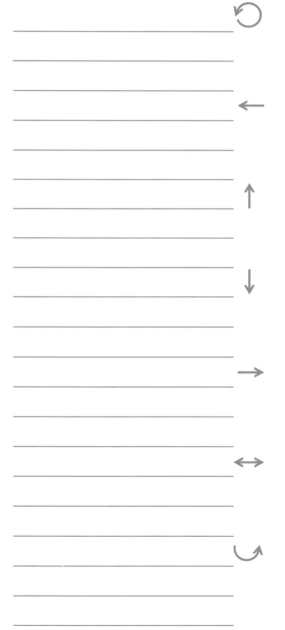

HOSEA 3

↺ _____
_____
_____
← _____
_____
_____
_____
↑ _____
_____
_____
↓ _____
_____
_____
→ _____
_____
_____
_____
↔ _____
_____
_____
_____
↰ _____
_____
_____

Hosea pictures God's love in a way that's virtually unforgettable—God told Hosea to marry Gomer, a prostitute. After she left him for other men, Hosea pursued Gomer continually to reclaim her as his wife. Though she committed adultery over and over, God told Hosea not to give up on her. Hosea's refusal to abandon his wife is a demonstration of the way God loves His people. Adultery presents a physical picture of sin. God has claimed His people as a husband claims his bride, and they are meant to be one. In our sin, however, people pursue other loves and abandon God. God's love is shown by His response to our adultery—He does not abandon us. Instead, He pursues us when we're unfaithful, inviting us back into a restored relationship. God proved His unfailing love to Israel and Judah, and through Jesus, He continues to love adulterers like you and me as well.

2 KINGS 17:6-23

The last half of 2 Kings and 2 Chronicles records the fall of Israel and Judah. God had reached His limit, and the time of judgment came. God used Assyria, one of Israel's enemies, to capture Samaria, which was the capital of the northern kingdom. Many Israelites died in the fighting, and others were exiled to live outside of the promised land in pagan nations. It was a terrible fate for God's people. Had they upheld their covenant commitment and been faithful to God, they could have lived in peace and experienced God's goodness in the promised land. But like Adam in the garden, they were expelled from the land to live as exiles. God made it clear why He acted in this way—the people had continually rebelled and worshiped other gods. They failed to reflect God's image, choosing instead to fill the earth with sin and brokenness. God had to act. The people mocked His name with their actions, and the exile was further proof that God would not overlook ongoing, unrepentant rebellion.

What does this passage say?

What did this passage mean to its original audience?

What does this passage tell us about God?

What does this passage tell us about man?

What does this passage demand of me?

How does this passage change the way I relate to people?

What does this passage prompt me to pray to God?

DAY 157

2 KINGS 22:8-20

↺ _____

_____

← _____

_____

_____

↑ _____

_____

↓ _____

_____

_____

→ _____

_____

_____

↔ _____

_____

_____

↰ _____

_____

_____

The northern kingdom of Israel experienced judgment before the southern tribes. However, this does not imply that Judah was somehow less sinful. In fact, their situation was so bad that 2 Kings reveals that the people didn't even know where a copy of God's law was. Hilkiah, a priest in the temple, found the book of the law and gave it to the king. The priest read God's Word and the people were confronted with their sinfulness. The law of God served as a mirror, revealing the impoverished state of the nation. The people wept over their sin. How could this happen? How could the people of God lose God's Word? The same way we do today—they were so intent on building their lives and pursuing their false gods that they forgot about God and His Word.

2 KINGS 23

Though the nation was unraveling and on the brink of destruction, we see glimmers of hope in kings like Josiah. After hearing God's law, Josiah led a number of reforms designed to restore the proper worship of God. He reminded the people of their covenant with God, reinstated the Passover celebration, and restored the temple to its proper function. He also destroyed the sites where Israel was prone to worship false gods. Josiah's actions demonstrate the bravery required to walk with God and point others to Him in a time of rampant sin. We know that Josiah's actions were critical—if the people did not repent and return to God, they would face exile as well. Christians today face a similar challenge. In a world marked by sin, we're called to walk faithfully with God and call others to obedience. Such faithfulness is vital for us to fulfill our God-given mission as image-bearers. Like Josiah, this type of faithfulness will require courage and conviction.

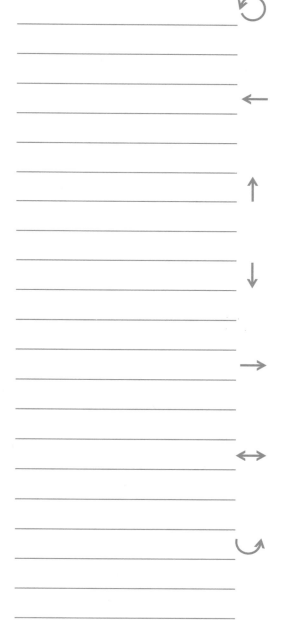

2 KINGS 24:10-17

↺ _____

_____

_____

← _____

_____

_____

↑ _____

_____

_____

↓ _____

_____

_____

→ _____

_____

_____

↔ _____

_____

_____

↪ _____

_____

_____

In spite of temporary reforms, the handwriting was on the wall. Israel fell to the Assyrians in 722 BC, and in 586 BC, the Babylonians defeated Judah as well. The exile should come as no surprise now that we've traced God's story through the Old Testament. He gave them warning after warning, yet the people consistently spurned His wisdom, instead pursuing their own ways. Notice that in both cases God used foreign nations to execute judgment on His people. Though the Assyrians and Babylonians did not worship the one true God, they still served God's purposes. He used those nations to crush His people, and this proves God is sovereign and in control of everything. He can use anyone or anything to accomplish His plan. Once again, God's people were in shambles. Would He leave them to die in exile, or would He continue to enact His plan to save them once and for all?

JOHN 2:13-25

Little changed by the time Jesus began His ministry. The temple, designed to be the dwelling place of God with His people and the site of worship, had become a marketplace. People still came to offer sacrifices, but they did this out of religious obligation rather than humble worship. The exchange of animals for sacrifice had become a money-making scheme for the religious leaders of the day. Jesus performed an exile of His own, driving the leaders out of the temple. He was appalled at the state of worship among the people of His day. They had no idea that, in the person of Jesus Christ, God literally dwelled among His people. Later, Jesus warned the leaders that they could destroy the temple of His body on the cross, but He would rise again after three days. From that point on, proper worship would no longer require a temple, but would instead depend on faith in Jesus and His sacrificial work.

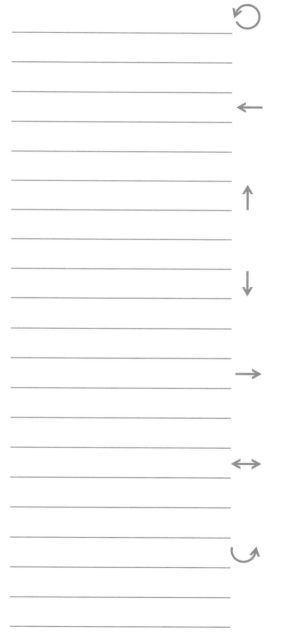

DANIEL 1

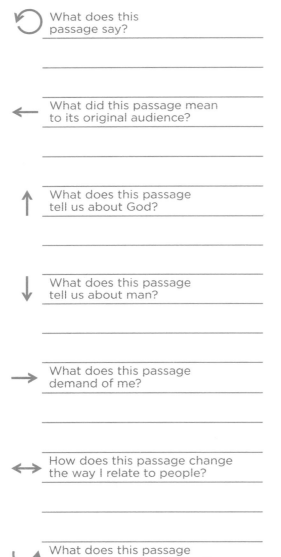

What does this passage say?

_____

_____

What did this passage mean to its original audience?

_____

_____

What does this passage tell us about God?

_____

_____

What does this passage tell us about man?

_____

_____

What does this passage demand of me?

_____

_____

How does this passage change the way I relate to people?

_____

_____

What does this passage prompt me to pray to God?

_____

_____

The prophets Daniel and Ezekiel addressed God's people during their time in exile. It's amazing that God even spoke to His people when they should have been receiving the silent treatment. They'd had plenty of warnings by this point and were experiencing the result of their rebellion. But God continued to sustain them, even in exile, and provided them with gracious words of hope for the future. The later portion of the book of Daniel speaks of the end of times, when God will defeat Satan, sin, and death forever. The early chapters of the book show God's faithfulness to men like Daniel while in exile. The Babylonian king made every effort to dismantle the faith of the Israelite exiles, even changing their names to represent the worship of false gods. Daniel stood strong, refusing to give in to the onslaught of forces trying to turn his heart away from God. The nation of Israel was never able to resist the worship of false gods—at least not for long—but Daniel showed that a deep faith in God's promises was sufficient to fight the world's sinfulness and remain obedient to God.

DANIEL 6

A lion's den was an appropriate picture for the challenge faced by the nation of Israel. Kicked out of the promised land, they lived in a hostile environment. Daniel was incapable of withstanding the lions alone, but the presence of God was with him in the den. The picture was clear—God had not abandoned His people, even when they were in exile in a foreign land. He was standing by their side to guard, protect, and preserve them, and they would never be permanently destroyed. Those who trust God as Daniel did will find that the steadfast love of God is never removed from His people. Even in judgment, God demonstrates His care and faithfulness to His promises. This provides hope for all who experience the consequences of sin. God does not turn His back on us in our sin, but He turns His face to us in love. He is with us, an ever-present help in times of trouble.

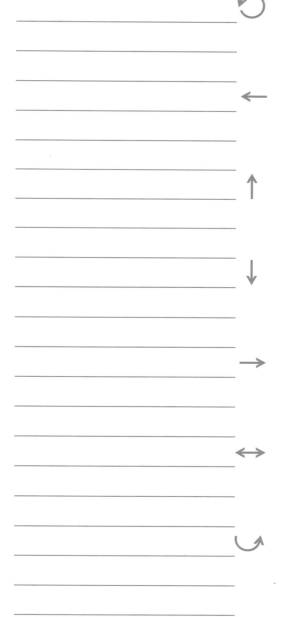

DAY 163

EZEKIEL 36:22-38

↺ _____

_____

_____

← _____

_____

_____

↑ _____

_____

_____

↓ _____

_____

_____

→ _____

_____

_____

↔ _____

_____

_____

↪ _____

_____

_____

Ezekiel, writing during the exile, pictured a future day when the fortunes of God's people would be changed. You might think this means they will regain the promised land, have a new king, or achieve victory over their enemies. The problem with any of these outcomes is that we already know what happens when they do—over and over God's people rebel and face judgment. The problem is far bigger than exile—it's sin! One way to understand God's plan in the Bible is to notice who actually causes the things that happen. In this short passage from the prophets, we read the word "I" over and over again. God does the work in this passage, and He will get glory for His name by working on behalf of His people to cleanse them from their sin. He will do this by removing their heart of stone—one that consistently rebels from God—and replacing it with a heart of flesh that longs to worship God. These future promises are the only hope for people who can't stop sinning.

EZEKIEL 37:1-14

God often helped His prophets to understand His plan through visions. The valley of dry bones clearly portrayed the way God promised to bring Israel back from exile, making it one of the most well-known visions in the Bible. As in creation, God brought life by speaking His Word. Though it appeared that the nation of Israel was dead, God would bring them back to life. This vision provides hope, not just for the nation of Israel, but for all who are dead in trespasses and sins. There is no way for a dead man to do anything to bring himself back to life—that person must be brought to life by someone more powerful than death. This is exactly what happens when someone comes to faith in Jesus. Jesus, who proved through His resurrection to be more powerful than death, brings people to life. Dry bones and dead sinners come to life by the power of God.

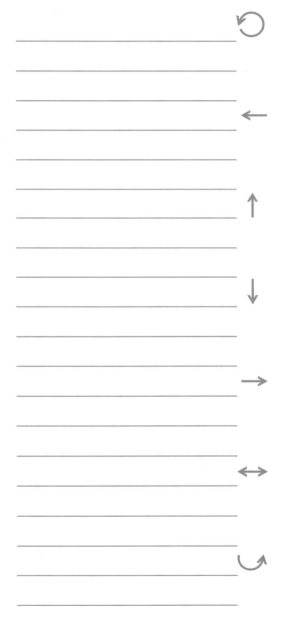

JOHN 11:38-44

↻ _____
_____
_____
← _____
_____
_____
↑ _____
_____
_____
↓ _____
_____
_____
→ _____
_____
_____
↔ _____
_____
_____
↰ _____
_____
_____

Both Jesus' humanity and divinity are pictured in the story of Lazarus. Jesus had friends He deeply loved. In fact, He loved them so much that when Lazarus died, Jesus wept when He saw the pain of Lazarus' sisters. Jesus is also God—the One with power over death, and with a word He can give new life to the dead. It's clear that the main point of the story wasn't really about Lazarus. After all, since Lazarus was human, even though he was brought back to life, he would one day die again. Jesus wanted His followers to see that He was God. In fact, when Jesus could have healed Lazarus, Jesus intentionally waited until Lazarus died so that the great glory of God could be shown. Imagine the story Lazarus had to tell for the rest of his life. He was dead and Jesus brought Him to life. If you are a Christian today, that's your story as well. You were once dead in your sin, and Jesus put His glory on display by bringing you to life.

NEHEMIAH 1

God promised to restore His people to the land as an act of grace. The Bible records the return of a small group of exiled Israelites to the promised land under Nehemiah and Ezra. The main goal of these leaders was to rebuild the city of Jerusalem and restore worship in the temple. It's painful to see how far the people fell. Their land was dismantled and the temple destroyed. The work that had taken them so long to complete had fallen into ruin. If there was ever a time when the fulfillment of God's promises looked bleak, this was the time. The temple's destruction served as a picture of a broken nation. Nehemiah worked to rebuild the city, and Ezra labored to restore worship. Yet the hope of the people was never found in a renewed land, but in the hope that God would somehow bring a permanent solution to their ongoing failure. As the people waited, Nehemiah and Ezra exemplified faithfulness and trust in God in the midst of great uncertainty.

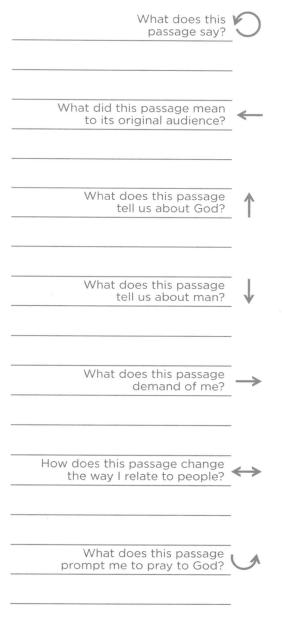

What does this passage say?

What did this passage mean to its original audience?

What does this passage tell us about God?

What does this passage tell us about man?

What does this passage demand of me?

How does this passage change the way I relate to people?

What does this passage prompt me to pray to God?

NEHEMIAH 8:1-8

↺ _____

_____

_____

← _____

_____

_____

↑ _____

_____

_____

↓ _____

_____

_____

→ _____

_____

_____

↔ _____

_____

_____

↪ _____

_____

_____

Ezra delivered a call to worship by reading God's Word in the presence of all of the people. You might imagine the significance of this moment. For years, these Israelites had been exiles in a foreign land where they had very little, if any at all, access to God's Word. At this point, they were back in the promised land and hearing clearly the Word of God once again. The religious leaders of the day did what pastors and church leaders do today. They stood before the people, read the Word of God, and explained it to the people so they could understand its meaning. Many of God's people today experience the privilege of having Bibles at home they can read in their own language. Preaching and teaching in the church helps support our personal time in God's Word and is a tool God uses to help us understand it. We should give praise to God when others guide us to know, understand, and apply His Word.

HAGGAI 1

If you wonder how the people handled the privilege of coming back to the land and working to rebuild the temple, then you need to look no further than Haggai 1. They returned and immediately built the foundation of the temple, but then they quit. For years, they did no other work on God's house because they were more intent on building their own houses. Rather than rebuking them directly, God simply asked them to consider their ways. How did things go when they put themselves first and neglected God and His purposes? The answer was clear. They worked hard but saw little fruit from their labor. They strived for blessing, but God would not give it. The only hope they had of prospering in the land was to do what God put them there to do in the first place—to reflect His image through their worship. The reality is that the very thing they longed for—the blessing of God—would only come if they pursued Him first. By seeking the blessing of God without really worshiping God, they missed both God and His blessing.

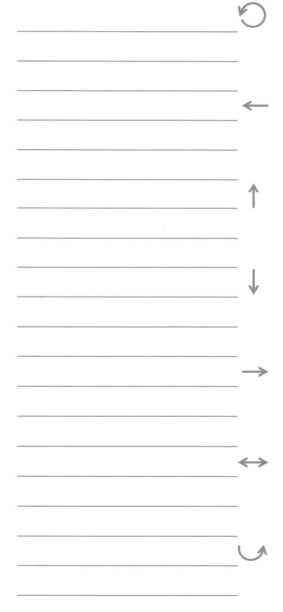

MALACHI 1:6-14

This is a fitting end to the Old Testament. After the book of Malachi, God would stop speaking through the prophets for over 400 years. Generations would come and go with no further word from the Lord. Before God's voice became quiet for a time, we were given one more picture of the state of worship among the people of God. You recall from the book of Leviticus that the people were expected to offer their very best, spotless animal to God in order to pay the price for their sins. In Malachi's day, the people continued to offer sacrifices, but rather than offering God their best, they chose animals that were about to die anyway. This way they could still feel good about themselves because they were offering some sacrifice, but they did it in a way that cost nothing. God was furious! Clearly, what was most important to God was not the sacrifice, but the hearts of His people. Half-hearted sacrifices proved that God didn't occupy their hearts, even after all He'd done for His people. Do the decades of silence that followed mean that God had finally had enough and given up on His promise?

LUKE 15:11-32

Jesus often told stories to communicate who He is and what He came to do. Luke 15 records three stories, or parables, that show how He loves sinners like us. The story of the two brothers in Luke 15 is more so the story of a father's great love. This man watched as his son took his inheritance and pursued a life of blatant sin. The consequences of his rebellion, like that of the nation of Israel, produced nothing but grief. In spite of the pain he felt, the father never gave up on his wayward child. He stood watching and waiting for him to repent and return to his father's loving care. The party that followed the son's return shows the extent of the father's love. Israel could have experienced the same type of celebration had they simply returned to God with their whole heart. But they didn't. God watched as they suffered the consequences of their rebellion, but He was never idle. The Father was actively waiting until just the right time when He would send the Promised One to find the wayward children and bring them back to the Father.

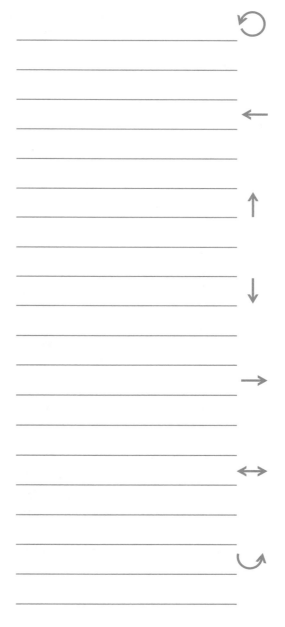

CHAPTER 7//JESUS

The entire Bible tells the story of Jesus. Though the name Jesus does not appear in the Old Testament, a clear picture was given starting all the way back at the beginning of our Bible concerning who Jesus would be and what He would do. You probably already knew that Jesus was important to the larger story of God long before you started reading this devotional, but you may not have understood exactly why. Now that we've journeyed through more than two-thirds of the Bible, it should be clear that Jesus was always God's plan to save sinners and fix a broken world.

The first four books of the New Testament, commonly referred to as the Gospels, describe Jesus' birth, life, death, and resurrection. Each author wrote to a unique audience, so he emphasized different aspects of Jesus' life. Along the way, Matthew, Mark, Luke, and John described the men and women who followed Jesus' teaching and His way of life. Their faith in Jesus set a pattern for all of us who call ourselves Christians today.

The primary focus of each Gospel centers on the death and resurrection of Jesus. In fact, Mark spent half of his book describing the final week of Jesus' life. It's clear that the Gospel writers believed Jesus was far more than an example of someone who lived a good life. If Jesus came just as a good example for us, then people would still be in a bind because their sin would make it impossible to follow the pattern Jesus set.

The most significant aspect of Jesus' work appears in His substitutionary death and victorious resurrection. In these acts, Jesus fulfilled the plan of God made in the garden and makes it possible for sinful men and women to be restored to a right relationship with God. Jesus is God's promise in a person.

There's no way any of us could write God's story. Try as we might, we would never be able to devise a plan through which the impossible price of sin would be paid and sinners forgiven. Thankfully we are not the ones writing the story—God is. He's been crafting all the details since the foundation of the world and working to make each chapter of the story happen just as He designed. Jesus proves that God always knows what He's doing.

MATTHEW 1:6-17

Beginning a book with a genealogy (and the entire New Testament) may seem strange. Matthew, writing to an audience descending from the ancient Israelites, believed the details of this genealogy were the most important clues to who Jesus is and what He came to do. The focus of the genealogy is on two individuals: Abraham and David. Now that you have a solid grasp of the story of the Old Testament, you should know why. Both Abraham and David received the covenant promises from God, through which God described His plan to save sinners and fix the world. God told both Abraham and David that the One who would come to fulfill these promises would emerge through their families. The fact that Jesus came from the line of Abraham and David proves that Jesus is the answer to God's plan. Along the way, Matthew also listed other various individuals through whom God brought Jesus to the world. This group contains the names of some prominent figures, some notorious sinners, and some people we know nothing about. God proves that no one is beyond the reach of His mission in the world.

What does this passage say?

What did this passage mean to its original audience?

What does this passage tell us about God?

What does this passage tell us about man?

What does this passage demand of me?

How does this passage change the way I relate to people?

What does this passage prompt me to pray to God?

LUKE 1:67-80

Zechariah's prophecy is a summary of the story of the Old Testament. Because God's Spirit filled him, Zechariah uniquely understood that Jesus would be the answer to every promise made by God. First up, John the Baptist would come before Jesus and prepare the people for His birth. John would be the last in a long line of people God raised up to point forward to the coming of Jesus. Zechariah referred to God's covenant—the promise He made with Israel beginning in Genesis. Remember, this covenant promise was not based on the obedience of Israel, but God pledged His love to the nation and committed to bring about a plan for their salvation. Beginning with John and then through Jesus, God would break the silence of the past 400 years with the birth of His Promised One. Sadly, the ones who should have been looking for Jesus' coming would reject Him and miss His offer of salvation.

LUKE 2:1-21

Jesus was born in the city David, and angels declared His identity right from the start. Even as a baby lying in a manger, Jesus was actually the Savior of the world. Through Him, God brought salvation to His people. Jesus is also the Christ, a word which means "anointed One." Like a king in the Old Testament, He was chosen by God to lead His people. And He is the Lord, the one who deserves the allegiance of all people. The angels, knowing all this, praised the glory of God. They knew of God's greatness, and the fulfillment of His promises to His people only heightened the sense of His glory. Once the shepherds saw Jesus, they also sang of the glory of God and told others about the Savior. Even today, those who know and love Jesus give glory to God for the hope He offers by telling others of His saving work.

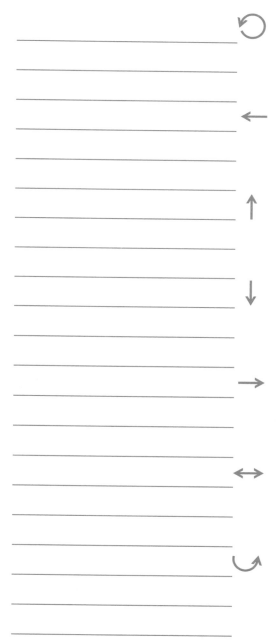

MATTHEW 2

↻ _____

_____

← _____

_____

↑ _____

_____

↓ _____

_____

_____

→ _____

_____

↔ _____

_____

_____

↰ _____

_____

_____

God protected Jesus in much the same way as He protected the firstborn children of Israel at the time of the Passover. A jealous king wanted Jesus dead, but God took care of His Promised One by providing a way of escape through Egypt. God delivered His Son, like the nation of Israel, from Egypt and brought Jesus out to begin His saving work. Each of these steps in Jesus' life was perfectly predicted by the prophets of God writing in the Old Testament. They knew the location of Jesus' birth and the place where He would live at the outset of His ministry. Not only are the details predicted by God, but they are designed by God as another way to show who Jesus is. Jesus' life followed the pattern of the nation of Israel, but there was a major difference. Jesus effectively accomplished what Israel was never able to do—His life perfectly reflects God's image to the world.

GALATIANS 4:1-7

Paul compared the relationship between people and God in the Old Testament to the relationship between slaves and slave masters. Slaves must obey the master's rules, and when they don't, they're punished. This type of relationship provides little hope for people who keep sinning, so God changed the nature of the relationship. At just the right time, God sent Jesus to the world. He was born under the old pattern, but He obeyed God completely. Faith in Jesus frees slaves from the burden of the law because they trust in Jesus, who obeyed the law on their behalf. They become sons, not slaves. As sons, all God's people from every nation receive the benefit of every promise God made to His people. The blessings God promised to Abraham, Isaac, Jacob, and David are given to all those who have faith in Jesus' perfect life, sacrificial death, and victorious resurrection.

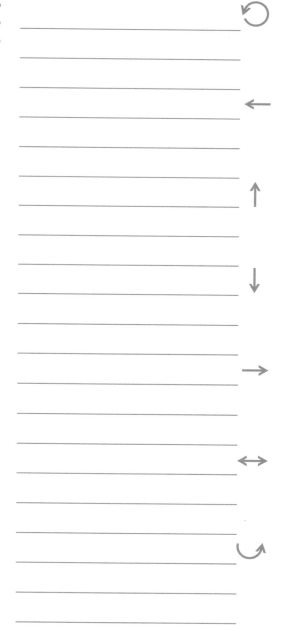

MATTHEW 4:12-22

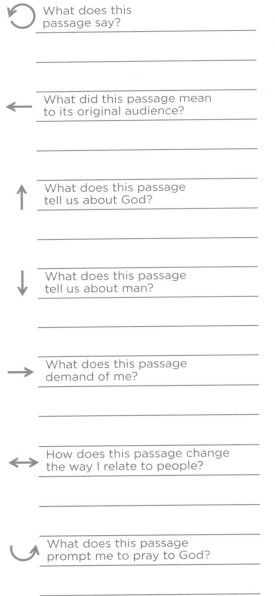

What does this
passage say?

_____

_____

What did this passage mean
to its original audience?

_____

_____

What does this passage
tell us about God?

_____

_____

What does this passage
tell us about man?

_____

_____

What does this passage
demand of me?

_____

_____

How does this passage change
the way I relate to people?

_____

_____

What does this passage
prompt me to pray to God?

_____

_____

Little is known about Jesus' childhood. The stories of the Bible fast-forward to the time when He began His ministry around the age of thirty. His message was simple—the kingdom God promised is here, now turn from your sin and follow Me. Jesus pursued an assortment of men and invited them to follow Him in a special way. This group, known as the disciples, journeyed with Jesus over the next three years. They watched as Jesus preached about His kingdom and demonstrated His great power. They even had the privilege of representing Jesus by doing powerful acts as well. The first step for the disciples was a simple act of faith. God called them, and they responded by willingly leaving behind their old lives to follow Jesus. God continues to call men and women to give up comfort, power, money, position, or anything else that might hinder them from wholeheartedly following after Him.

MARK 3:13-19

Mark listed the names of some of Jesus' earliest followers. Throughout God's story, there have always been an assortment of people He's chosen to be a part of His mission, and the disciples were no different. They weren't selected based on the fact that they were somehow superior or more holy than others. God simply called them as an act of grace. Mark mentioned two unique benefits these men experienced. First, they were called to be with God. Of all the people on the planet, these men got to walk and talk with the Son of God. They had a front row seat to the life and ministry the One who is the exact imprint of God's image. Second, they were sent to do the works of God. By virtue of the fact that they were with Jesus and filled with His power, they were sent to work on His behalf, and they represented God through their words and actions. These two things—being with God and doing what God desires—go hand and hand. The more we live in intimacy with God, the better we are able to represent Him through our lives.

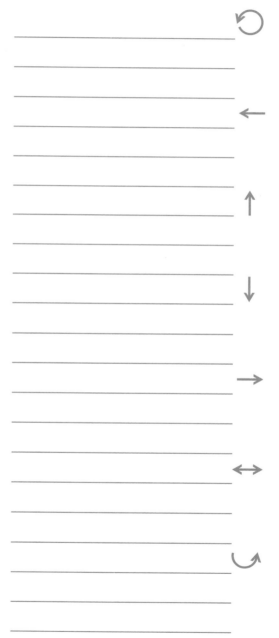

MATTHEW 16:24-28

The disciples received some challenging words from Jesus as they followed Him. He made it clear that He is to be the most important part of people's lives. Nothing, not even burying a dead relative, is to be more important than Jesus. Everything else pales in comparison to loving Jesus and doing what He says. This is not simply true for the disciples, it's also true for anyone who wants to follow Jesus, including you and me. Jesus said that all those who want to follow Him must die to their selfish desires in order to follow Him. A cross is an appropriate picture for the life of those who love Jesus. Not only did Jesus die on the cross, but all those who follow Jesus in faith must also die to themselves in order to live the life God desires.

JOHN 1:35-51

John truly recognized Jesus. In this time in history, there was no shortage of religious leaders seeking young followers. Rabbis, or teachers, were very common, but Jesus was different than other rabbis of His day. He was not simply a good, religious teacher—He was the Lamb of God! John's description makes sense after we've seen God's plan through the Old Testament sacrificial system. The Israelites were required to offer a perfect lamb as a substitute for their sins, and that lamb would die in their place. The problem with the old way was, as we have seen, that the people had to continually offer these sacrifices because they kept sinning. Jesus came as a final sacrifice, the perfect Lamb to atone for the sins of His people forever. Everyone who follows Jesus knows Him, like John did, as the Lamb of God who takes away their sin.

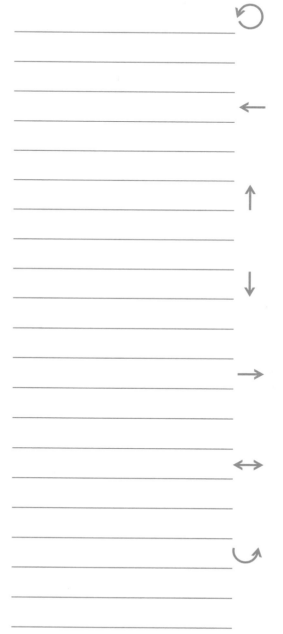

ROMANS 1:1-7

↺ _____

_____

← _____

_____

↑ _____

_____

↓ _____

_____

→ _____

_____

↔ _____

_____

↰ _____

_____

Jesus didn't only call the twelve disciples to follow Him, there were hundreds of other followers with Him during His ministry. This included many of those He healed, a host of women, and a few prominent apostles. And the list of those who followed Jesus does not stop there. Paul wrote that the church was filled with those who followed Jesus. They began their journey of faith in much the same way as the first disciples—called by God. Those who live after Jesus' earthly ministry aren't called in exactly the same way—we don't see Jesus or hear His voice the way the first disciples did. Yet God still speaks to us through His Word and calls us to belong to Him. Those who respond to this call by faith are saved. Paul went further to say he was called in a unique way to take the message of the gospel to those who hadn't yet heard. Like Paul, Christians are called to faith in Jesus that we would share the good news of His work to a lost world.

MATTHEW 5:1-12

Matthew recorded an extended passage of Jesus' teaching, commonly known as the Sermon on the Mount. Jesus began this sermon by pointing His hearers to the blessings of God, a common theme in the Old Testament. Starting with Abraham, God said His people would receive the blessing of God and would in turn serve as a blessing to others. Jesus provided a description of the type of people who were blessed, including those who mourn, those who seek peace, and those who are persecuted. It is clear that the blessing of God does not necessarily mean wealth, power, or fame. The blessings God offers are ultimately forgiveness of sins and a restored relationship with Him. This is true blessedness. The people who understand that God's blessing comes through faith are able to face sufferings, unrest, pain, and loss knowing that they've received God's blessings in Christ, and nothing in the world can take that blessing away.

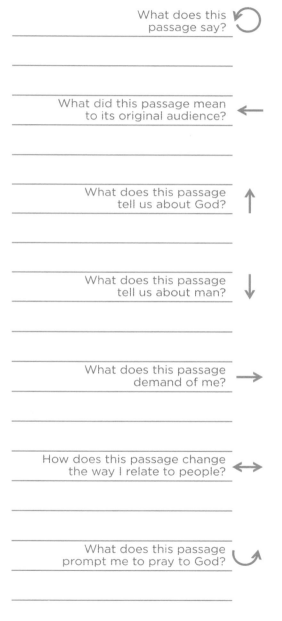

What does this passage say?

What did this passage mean to its original audience?

What does this passage tell us about God?

What does this passage tell us about man?

What does this passage demand of me?

How does this passage change the way I relate to people?

What does this passage prompt me to pray to God?

MATTHEW 5:17-20

↺ _____

_____

← _____

_____

_____

↑ _____

_____

↓ _____

_____

_____

→ _____

_____

_____

↔ _____

_____

↪ _____

_____

Throughout the Sermon on the Mount, Jesus did something interesting with the Old Testament law. He did not throw it out, but instead He intensified it. He said the issue isn't just that people commit murder, but that their hearts rage with anger. It isn't simply that couples commit adultery, it's that their hearts burn with lust. They don't just break promises, but they lie and deceive. There's no way people can ever clean up their sinful hearts on their own, which is why Jesus' statement in this passage is so important—He is the fulfillment of the law. He came to obey God perfectly. He never became sinfully angry, much less murdered. He never sinned through His actions, or even in His thoughts or motives. Jesus is perfect, and He accomplished what Adam, Israel, and we today could never do. As a gift of grace, God gives those who trust in Jesus perfect standing before God. God sees those who have faith in Jesus as if they had kept the law perfectly, because Jesus fulfilled the law on their behalf.

MARK 4:1-20

A common way Jesus taught others about who He is and what He came to do was through parables, which are short stories designed to communicate one central point. Jesus used the parable of the sower to illustrate the message He and the disciples would communicate about the kingdom of God. They would sow the seed widely, but only a small percentage of people would respond in faith. This parable reminds Jesus' disciples that the work we do is not in vain. God faithfully uses the few who respond in faith to produce an abundant harvest of godly fruit. The disciples themselves would demonstrate this reality. Beginning with a small band of disciples who followed Him by faith, Jesus would transform the world. This parable provides hope for all who share the good news of Jesus with others. Though many will reject His message of salvation, some will hear the message of Jesus and trust in His work. We can depend on God to bring salvation as we are faithful to scatter the seed.

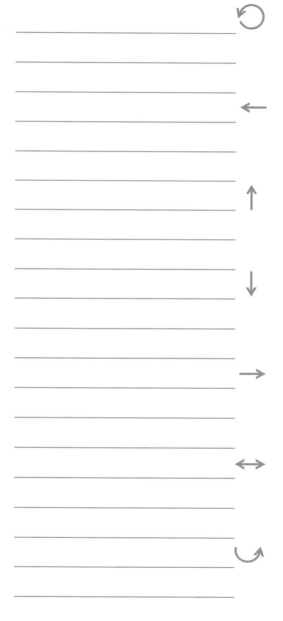

MARK 6:1-6

Among those who did not respond in faith are many of the Jews, or descendants of the ancient Israelites. You'd think that the Jewish people would have been the first to trust in Jesus. They'd seen the benefit of the promises of God, the Word of God, and the sacrificial system. The prophets pointed them to the day Jesus would come, the time when God would fulfill His promises by sending the Savior. Jesus simply did not fit their perception of what this Savior would do. He was, after all, just a carpenter from the obscure village of Nazareth. Even those in His hometown didn't believe He was who He said He was. The people who had the most exposure to Him and His message were the ones who failed to have faith. Too often, the same is true in our day. Many have access to Bibles, churches on every corner, and friends who talk to them about the good news. Some believe they are saved simply because they've heard about Jesus all their lives. But like the Jews, these people often fail to know Jesus by placing their faith in Him.

GALATIANS 2:15–3:14

Paul expressed his anger at the church in Galatia. At the heart of his frustration was the fact that the Christians in this church were slowly falling back into their old pattern of life. They based their standing before God in their ability to keep the law. It was becoming common in the church for people to believe they had to be circumcised or keep certain dietary laws in order to be saved. Paul reminded them that this was not the good news of Jesus. The gospel message declared that Jesus fulfilled the law on behalf of sinners, and faith in His work is what makes someone right with God. No one can earn God's favor by keeping the law. Paul said the church was in danger of undermining the very nature of grace through their actions. Grace is God's favor given to those He saves, even though they do nothing to earn His kindness. By striving to keep the law in order to be saved, they were indicating that they believed their salvation was based, at least in part, on their actions. Paul reminds us that Jesus did everything so we can rest in His grace.

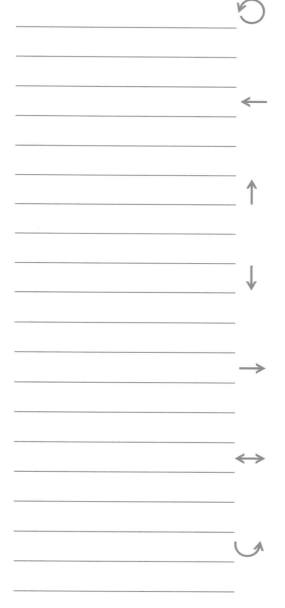

MARK 2:1-12

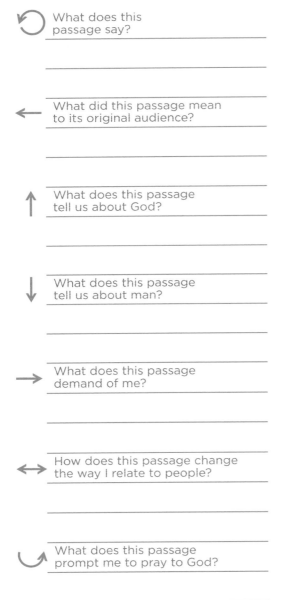

What does this
passage say?

What did this passage mean
to its original audience?

What does this passage
tell us about God?

What does this passage
tell us about man?

What does this passage
demand of me?

How does this passage change
the way I relate to people?

What does this passage
prompt me to pray to God?

Healing shows up again and again as a large part of Jesus' ministry. Each of the four Gospel writers described a number of examples where Jesus healed someone who was blind, lame, deaf, demon-possessed, or even dead. The story of the paralytic underscores the power of Jesus. He was widely known as a healer, so much so that the friends of the paralyzed man would do anything to get him to Jesus. Jesus recognized their faith in His power—that they went to all the trouble to lower their friend through the roof was a picture of their faith. Jesus didn't immediately heal the man, however. First, He forgave his sins. The religious leaders were furious—only God can forgive sins! This is exactly Jesus' point. He is God and His healings are a way to show the world the power He possesses.

LUKE 8:26-39

The demon-possessed man showed another example of Jesus' power over both the physical and spiritual realm. This man's situation was dire. He was a mess and everyone knew it. Others had tried to help him, or at least contain him, but they had no luck. Everything changed when the man met Jesus. The demons immediately recognized Jesus as the Son of God, and they trembled. Jesus spoke, and the demons fled—with a word, He did what no one else could. The formerly demon-possessed man sat at the feet of Jesus in awe and worship. Jesus didn't leave the man there. He commanded him to go back to his home and tell everyone all that God had done. Can you imagine what the town must have thought when they saw this man coming? He certainly didn't have the best reputation, but Jesus had changed everything, and the man's transformed life was used to point others to the glory of God.

JOHN 9

↺ _____
_____
← _____
_____
_____
↑ _____
_____
↓ _____
_____
_____
→ _____
_____
_____
↔ _____
_____
_____
↪ _____
_____
_____

In another healing story, Jesus encountered a man born blind. The common assumption in Jesus' day was that someone in this situation had surely done something to deserve it. Either his sin or someone else's sin caused him to experience this blindness. Jesus disagreed. Broken people live in a broken world—that's just life. Jesus didn't blame the blindness on anyone, but instead, He used this man's brokenness to point others to the greatness of God. The man's testimony was simple, yet profound—*"I was blind, and now I can see."* This is the same story all Christians can tell. We were born in a state of sin and brokenness. There was nothing we could do to fix ourselves, but Jesus took our pain and made us whole. He made us see both our sin and our need for a Savior, and because of His grace, we see clearly the glory of God. Now we live so that others can see His glory as well.

LUKE 7:1-17

An interesting thing about these healings is that the ones healed are not the primary focus of the story. Both the centurion and the widow experienced the grace of God in response to their faith. In fact, their faith was so great that Jesus marveled. Many people marveled at Jesus throughout His life, but this time, He was the one who was awestruck. Faith gets Jesus' attention. There's no doubt that Jesus has the power to heal anyone of anything at anytime He pleases. But He doesn't heal everyone. For example, He did very few miracles in His hometown of Nazareth. Why? Jesus performed miracles to help people come to faith, and the people in Jesus' hometown weren't open to believing in Him as the Messiah. When we learn of Jesus' claims to be God and His offer of salvation, the only appropriate response is to have faith, just like the centurion and the widow. He saves those who have faith that He is Who He says He is, and that He has the power to deliver us from sin and death.

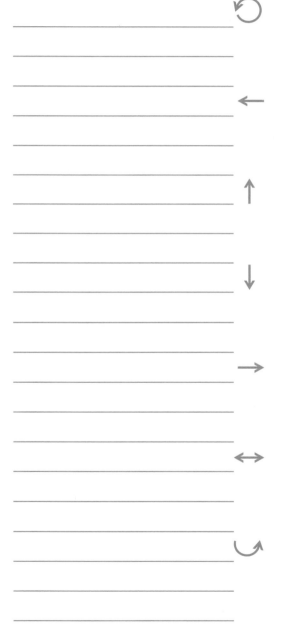

1 CORINTHIANS 15:35-58

Paul encouraged the church in Corinth by explaining how Jesus' resurrection foretells what will happen to all those who have faith in His work. The human body, though it will die on this earth, will rise to new life with God forever. This new body will not be like the former one. It will not grow old, get sick, or fall apart. It will be a spiritual body that will be whole and healthy. Christians will be raised from the dead like Jesus was raised from the dead. They will also be healed like those Jesus healed. The miracles Jesus performed remind us of the past—there was a time in the garden when the human body didn't suffer in a sin-filled world. Miracles also point forward to the future when our bodies will be healed of every sickness and disease. Our current bodies are not our final home. We live in them for the short time we're on earth, but we can look forward to the day God will give us new, glorified bodies.

JOHN 3:1-21

The Gospels provide a number of memorable stories describing salvation in vivid detail. You're likely familiar with one of the verses from Jesus' interaction with a Pharisee named Nicodemus. This ruler knew Jesus was special because he'd heard Jesus' teaching and had seen His miracles. Jesus told Nicodemus that He couldn't know God or enter His kingdom unless he was born again. This image was strange to Nicodemus, who questioned how someone could be reborn as an adult. Jesus isn't speaking of physical birth—He's speaking of spiritual rebirth. Because of Adam's sin, the first birth enters us into a life of slavery to sin which ultimately results in death. Jesus offers a new birth through faith that enters us into a life of worship to God. The offer of new life is possible because God loved His children so much that He gave Jesus on our behalf. Whoever believes—regardless of their past mistakes or failures—can enter the kingdom of God by faith in Jesus.

What does this passage say?

What did this passage mean to its original audience?

What does this passage tell us about God?

What does this passage tell us about man?

What does this passage demand of me?

How does this passage change the way I relate to people?

What does this passage prompt me to pray to God?

JOHN 4:1-30

In Jesus' time on earth, no one would ever expect to see a Jewish man speaking with a Samaritan woman—much less a woman with such a colorful past. The woman at the well came in search of water, but the true need was in her heart. Jesus knew her sin, as well as the guilt and shame she experienced. The well appropriately pictured what was happening in her heart. She was trying to fill the thirst of her heart by repeatedly lowering herself into sin, but sin could never quench her thirst. Jesus offered her an alternative. She could come to Him and never thirst again, because He is a well of living water that will never run dry. Her options mirror ancient Israel, who had the offer of living water, but instead chose to dig their own cisterns that couldn't hold water. This woman had been digging cisterns all her life, but she encountered the source of living water, and He offered her eternal salvation. She walked back into town, no longer a broken woman looking for satisfaction, but a woman who had been transformed by Jesus' offer of life.

LUKE 9:10-17

In Samaria, Jesus used water to point a sinful woman to salvation. Here, He used food to do the same thing. Jesus' disciples were unsure how to feed the large crowds that had gathered, but Jesus wasn't worried. He took five loaves of bread and a couple of fish to feed all 5,000 men, plus the women and children. Not only did Jesus feed them, but the food never ran out. The people ate until they were all full, and there were leftovers. The twelve disciples each filled a basket of the remaining food, which are probably symbolic of the way God provided food for the twelve tribes of Israel during their time in the wilderness. God continued giving them food—this time through His Son, Jesus. Soon Jesus would break bread again to show what would happen to His body, which was broken on a Roman cross. Jesus' body provides salvation to all those who trust Him in faith. Those who do will have the hunger of their souls eternally satisfied.

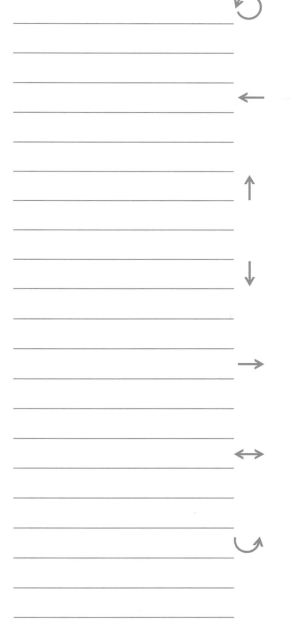

JOHN 10:1-21

Jesus used another familiar image to describe His love for His people and His mission in the world. Like a shepherd who lives to care for His sheep, Jesus lives to care for His people. He's not like a robber or a thief, who hurt the sheep and lead them to destruction. He's a good shepherd who strives to lead them to places they can thrive and be safe from harm. Jesus loves His sheep so much that He lays down His life for them. No one can take Jesus' life from Him, but He gave it up willingly for the salvation of His sheep, in Israel and the nations. Those who know Him as their shepherd—who hear His voice—will be gathered together into one flock with Jesus as the Great Shepherd. They will follow Him and experience the abundant life He created His people to experience.

PSALM 23

God uses the imagery of shepherds and sheep to describe His mission, and the work of the great Shepherd described in John 10 is also seen in many places throughout the Old Testament. Psalm 23 beautifully pictures the work of the shepherd. At each movement in this Psalm, God is the primary One doing the work: He makes me lie down, He leads me, He goes with me, He comforts me, He prepares a table for me. The sheep get to experience the joy that comes from following a shepherd who loves them dearly and leads them faithfully. They have nothing to fear. Even though they may experience pain, the good Shepherd guides them, walking with them to ensure that they arrive at their destination safely. The good and merciful Shepherd is the ever-present companion of the sheep.

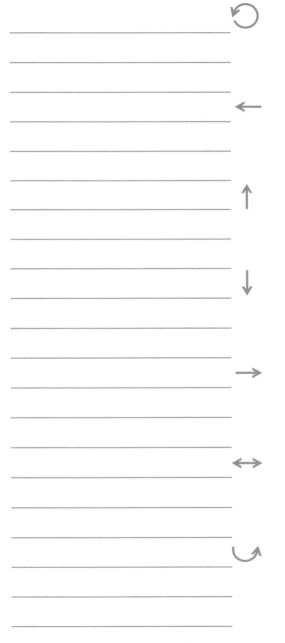

JOHN 1:29-34

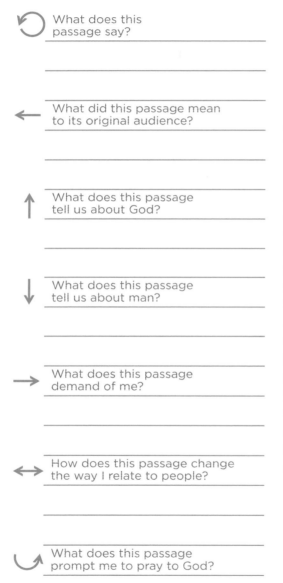

What does this
passage say?

_____

_____

← What did this passage mean
to its original audience?

_____

_____

↑ What does this passage
tell us about God?

_____

_____

↓ What does this passage
tell us about man?

_____

_____

→ What does this passage
demand of me?

_____

_____

↔ How does this passage change
the way I relate to people?

_____

_____

↪ What does this passage
prompt me to pray to God?

_____

_____

Many of those who met Jesus knew there was something special about Him. Not only did He speak with authority, but He was able to perform miracles proving His power. Unfortunately, many simply thought He was sent as a prophet or miracle-worker. They thought He was _from_ God, but did not believe He _was_ God. John, however, knew the truth. From the beginning, John knew God had chosen Jesus to atone for the sins of the world. Jesus would be the perfect and final sacrifice offered, so that the sins of God's people would be forgiven forever. God gave John supernatural eyes to see the presence of God in the person of Jesus Christ. Others lacked such faith and continually failed to see that Jesus is God, even in spite of everything He said and did. Jesus knew that it was not enough for people to believe He was a great man, excellent teacher, or incredible miracle worker. What mattered was whether or not people recognized that He is God.

JOHN 10:22-42

The Jewish leaders were at the top of the list of those who did not believe Jesus was God, even though they should have been the first to believe. Jesus made it clear that His works were meant to communicate one central truth—He and God the Father are one. Anyone who sees Jesus also sees God. Jesus is God with skin on. It's easy to condemn the Jewish leaders for their disbelief, but you might imagine how hard this was for them to believe. This son of Mary and Joseph, a carpenter from Nazareth, was God? Few would have expected God's promised One to come this way, but this was God's plan from the beginning of creation. Salvation hinged on whether or not people believed in this claim. If they believed Jesus is God, then they would be saved and protected forever. If they did not, they would perish. Simply stated, there was, and is, no other alternative.

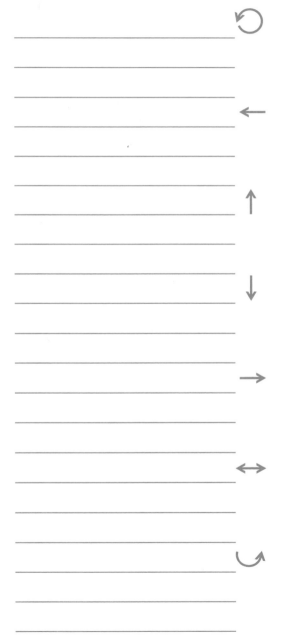

MATTHEW 8:23-27

Jesus demonstrated authority over every kind of human sickness and disease. He could fix everything broken in the human body. He also proved that He could fix everything broken in the world. Since sin entered creation, storms, hurricanes, tornadoes, and other disasters have pointed to the fact that something is not right in the world. Sin damaged creation itself, and it also needs to be made right. Jesus, the One who spoke all things into existence, calmed a raging storm with just a word. No one but God has that kind of power. The peace that followed the storm represents the healing of the created world that will come when Jesus returns and makes all things right again. Not only will the human body be perfect, but the world itself will be fixed. We will spend eternity in a perfect world that forever shows off the greatness of God.

MATTHEW 12:1-8

There is another way that Jesus showed the world He was God. Because they believed it was essential for a right relationship with God, many followed various aspects of the Old Testament law, and resting on the Sabbath day was very important. Any work was off limits, and the people created an extensive list of types of activity considered to be work. Jesus' act of healing on the Sabbath was considered a blatant disregard for the law. *Who did He think He was?* The answer is that Jesus knew He was God, the One who made the Sabbath and perfectly understood the God-given intent behind this law. He understood that the various man-made stipulations associated with the divine law missed the point. Because He wasn't merely a man, He held the authority to discount the human law in order to bring salvation and healing to this man. The religious leaders of Jesus' day clearly understood that Jesus believed He was God, a claim that would soon get Him killed.

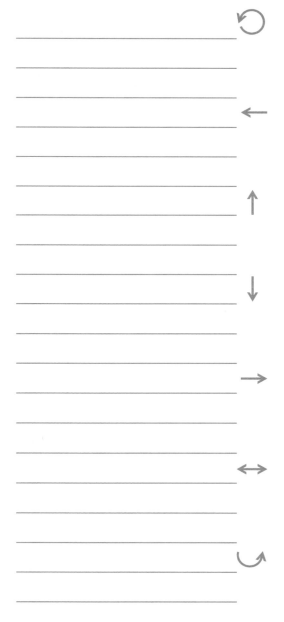

2 CORINTHIANS 13:11-14

↺ _____

_____

← _____

_____

↑ _____

_____

↓ _____

_____

→ _____

_____

↔ _____

_____

↪ _____

_____

In our day, it is common to meet people who have great respect for Jesus. They may think that He was a great leader, teacher, even miracle-worker. Jesus certainly embodied these things, but He was much more. No one experiences salvation because they believe Jesus was special—salvation comes to those who have faith in Jesus as God. Paul finished a section of his letter to the church at Corinth with a statement of the divinity of Jesus. In fact, He united all three members of the Trinity and described each of them as God: The Father is God. Jesus, the Son, is God. And the Holy Spirit is God, as well. While the word "Trinity" is not used in the Bible, undoubtedly the authors understood that the one true God consists of three persons who are each God and possess the full measure of God's glory.

MATTHEW 16:13-23

The cross was no surprise for Jesus. He knew it was coming. His followers, on the other hand, had a hard time grasping what Jesus told them about His impending death. Peter made a clear statement about who Jesus was and what He came to do. He is the Christ, the anointed One, sent by God to save sinners and fix the broken world. It took the disciples a long time to realize this truth, but Peter seemed to finally get it. However, Peter couldn't imagine that the Christ would suffer and die on a cross reserved for criminals. He'd been with Jesus and knew that Jesus never sinned. He didn't deserve to die, much less such a humiliating and brutal death on a cross. Jesus knew this was His fate—He was sent to die, and any opposition to this purpose was straight from Satan himself.

What does this passage say?

What did this passage mean to its original audience?

What does this passage tell us about God?

What does this passage tell us about man?

What does this passage demand of me?

How does this passage change the way I relate to people?

What does this passage prompt me to pray to God?

MATTHEW 23:1-15

↺ _____

_____

← _____

_____

↑ _____

_____

↓ _____

_____

→ _____

_____

↔ _____

_____

↪ _____

_____

Throughout Jesus' ministry, religious leaders were the most vocal opponents to His work. They harassed Him at every turn and undermined His claims to be God. Jesus took direct aim at one group of these opponents, the Pharisees, with a lengthy list of accusations. In contrast to the blessing He pronounced in the Sermon on the Mount, Jesus warned the Pharisees of their doom. The core of His condemnation focused on the Pharisees as frauds. Their outsides appeared to be holy, but their hearts oozed sin. They led others, but in the wrong direction—far away from God rather than toward Him. The hypocrisy of the Pharisees pictures an ever-present temptation for each of us. It's easy to do or say the right things without having a heart that loves Jesus. We can fool ourselves and others, but God sees clearly and He's not pleased with those who say they love God but live like they don't.

JOHN 11:45-57

It didn't take long for the leaders to determine that the best course of action was to get rid of Jesus. He threatened their way of life, openly criticized them, and performed miracles that could only come from God. Worse, there were huge crowds following Jesus. Knowing what's in the hearts and minds of all people, Jesus wasn't surprised by the religious leaders' plan to kill Him. However, it would happen according to God's purpose, and the timing of His death was His to determine. Jesus told the disciples that no one could take His life from Him—instead He would willingly lay it down. It's not as if some group of religious leaders could sneak up on Jesus and haul Him off to His death. Until the exact moment God had determined for Jesus to die, He lived freely. It might look like the leaders were setting a trap, but Jesus could not be caught by their plan.

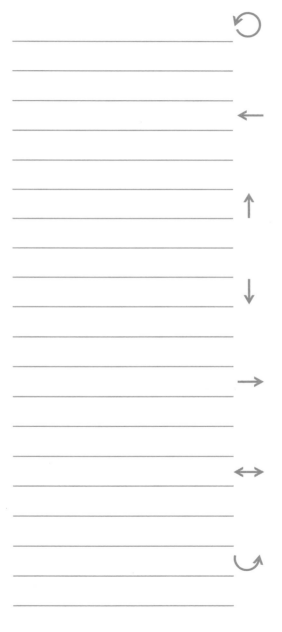

LUKE 19:28-40

↻ _____

_____

_____

← _____

_____

_____

↑ _____

_____

_____

↓ _____

_____

_____

→ _____

_____

_____

↔ _____

_____

_____

↪ _____

_____

_____

The details of Jesus' final week were predicted long ago by the prophets. They saw a coming day when the King of All would ride into Jerusalem on a donkey, willingly moving towards His death. By this time, there were many who wanted Jesus dead, and the end was certainly near. But as Jesus courageously entered Jerusalem, the disciples sang praises to His glory and greatness. They knew He was who He said, their song echoing the one sung over thirty years ago by the angels at His birth. Jesus brings peace to the earth, but not in the way many expected. Jesus is no political leader who restored Israel as a national powerhouse. The peace He came to bring was of another sort—Jesus' life and death made peace between sinful humans and the God of the universe.

HEBREWS 12:1-2

The final chapters of the book of Hebrews describe the outcome of a life of faith for those who have trusted in Jesus' finished work. You've probably noticed God doesn't simply take His people to heaven once they are saved. We continue to run the race of life that God created us to run, and it's our purpose to reflect God's image for the years He gives us to live on this earth. To do this, we are called to throw off the sin that slows us down and hinders our ability to run in a race that is certainly going to be long and difficult. The author of Hebrews said the best way to run the race is to look to Jesus. He's the perfect example of someone who had a difficult race to run. His race led Him straight to a brutal death on a Roman cross, but He went to the cross joyfully because He knew the prize waiting for Him at the end of His race. He would rise from the dead and return to the Father having completed the work God gave Him to do. In the same way, Christians can run the race of life by focusing on the future hope that is sure to come when our bodies are freed from sin, the world is no longer broken, and we can worship God forever.

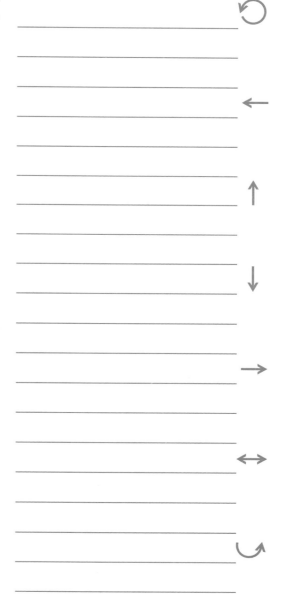

MATTHEW 26:17-29

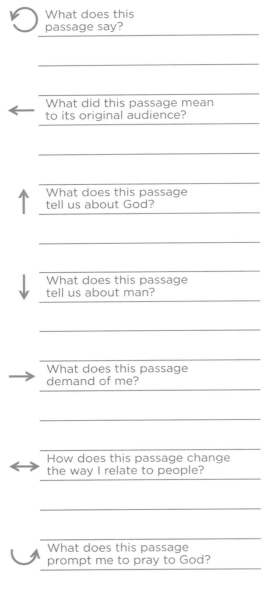

What does this passage say?

What did this passage mean to its original audience?

What does this passage tell us about God?

What does this passage tell us about man?

What does this passage demand of me?

How does this passage change the way I relate to people?

What does this passage prompt me to pray to God?

The Gospel writers spent a great deal of time describing the final days of Jesus' life, revealing this is centrally important to a proper understanding of Jesus. He was sent to die as the fulfillment of God's plan. Jesus knew this plan all along, continually reminding His disciples of what was to come. God used one disciple, Judas, to hand Jesus over to those who wanted Him dead. Prior to this betrayal, Jesus reminded His disciples of what the future held one final time. He took the bread and wine at the annual Passover meal and used it as a picture of His death. His body would be broken like the bread they tore to share and eat, and His blood would be poured out like the wine they would drink. This death would fulfill the new covenant promise God made to His people through the prophet Jeremiah. Those who had faith in Jesus' work would receive a new heart, allowing them to love God and reflect Him the way they were created.

LUKE 22:39-62

Jesus' prayer in the garden revealed the pain He faced. He knew His death would not be easy. In fact, it was the most heinous way a human could die. The pain was compounded by the fact that He would face the full wrath of God for the sins of the world, and He would feel, in a very real way, the anger of God for the first time. Jesus asked the Father if there was any way He could avoid drinking the cup of God's wrath—but He knew the Father's plan. As an act of humble submission, He committed Himself to God's will rather than His own desires. The disciples didn't have the same level of commitment. They couldn't even stay awake to pray. Peter— the one who recently called Jesus "the Christ"—even denied knowing Jesus. Thankfully God is not like people. People are short-sighted and selfish. However, God faithfully follows through on the plan made long ago and willingly keeps His promises, even when it causes Him pain.

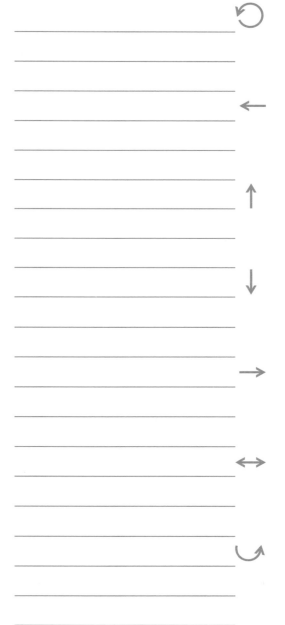

DAY 208

LUKE 23:18-56

↺ _____

_____

← _____

_____

↑ _____

_____

↓ _____

_____

→ _____

_____

↔ _____

_____

↪ _____

_____

The Lamb of God died. The human players in this story are men like Herod and Pilate, but the main character is God. He's the One who wrote this story and brought it to fulfillment in ways no one could have imagined. The Promised One hung on a tree—a vivid picture of the curse of God for human sin. Because of our sin—every selfish action, every corrupt thought, every desire for things God doesn't approve—we deserve this kind of death, and it should have been sinful people on the cross. But instead, it was the sinless Son of God who died. Even on the cross, Jesus looked beyond His pain and brought salvation to a criminal hanging by His side. Few would have imagined that this death would bring salvation to multitudes more in the years to follow. It's hard to imagine how a dead man in a tomb could bring salvation, but with the power of God nothing is impossible.

MATTHEW 27:45-66

Various signs accompanied the death of Jesus, none more significant than the temple veil being torn. Since the time of the tabernacle and the temple, the people were barred from God's presence, and a curtain hung between them and the altar of God. People could not approach God because His holiness would literally have destroyed them. Only a specific person—the High Priest—could enter behind the veil, and he could only enter at a specific time of the year after offering animal sacrifices. Jesus' death changed all that. God tore the veil in the temple from top to bottom showing that people could now approach God with confidence. Because of Jesus' perfect life and sinless death on their behalf, there was no longer a need for an earthly high priest or a veil to protect sinful people from God. Faith in Jesus is sufficient to cleanse our sin and make us holy, allowing us to enter the presence of God.

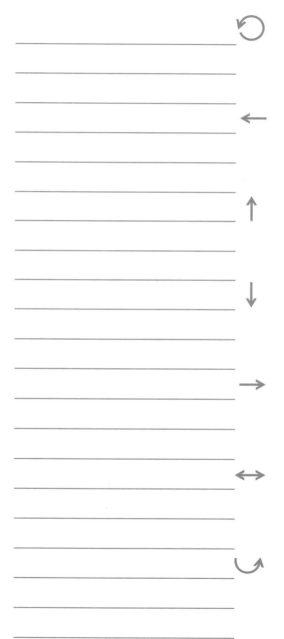

PHILIPPIANS 2:4-11

↺ _____
_____
_____
← _____
_____
_____
↑ _____
_____
_____
↓ _____
_____
_____
→ _____
_____
_____
↔ _____
_____
_____
↰ _____
_____
_____

This passage is one of the earliest known songs in the church. The story it tells can be imagined as two great mountains with a large valley in the middle. On the top of the first mountain stands Jesus prior to His life and death. He's with God, possessing every aspect of the glory of God. On the second mountain is Jesus after His death and resurrection. He's once again with God, and worshipers are gathered around His throne proclaiming His glory. In the middle lies the valley of Jesus' life and death. He willingly laid aside His glory with the Father, took on human flesh, and came to a broken world. The God of the universe became a servant and gave His life to pay for the sins of His people. This type of humility—this great love—is the reason He is worthy of our worship and praise.

MATTHEW 28:1-10

Death does not have the final word. Jesus did exactly what He told His disciples He would do—He gave up His life and defeated death on the third day. There's no indication that the women who went to Jesus' tomb that morning expected to find it empty. They were stunned like everyone else when they found their Master wasn't there. They'd given their lives to follow Jesus, and their hopes had been dashed and their dreams shattered. Not only had Jesus died, but His body was nowhere to be found. At the tomb, they were greeted by an angel with a common message. You would expect people who see an angel to be a bit afraid, but the angel's message brought great joy and hope—not fear. Jesus was alive, just as He promised! In fact, He was on the move again—going on ahead of the women to Galilee to continue the next stage of God's story.

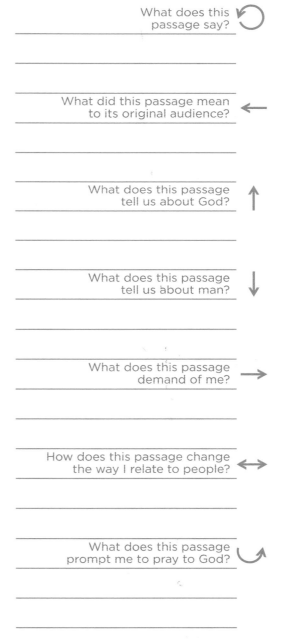

What does this
passage say?

_____

_____

_____

What did this passage mean
to its original audience?

_____

_____

What does this passage
tell us about God?

_____

_____

What does this passage
tell us about man?

_____

_____

What does this passage
demand of me?

_____

_____

How does this passage change
the way I relate to people?

_____

_____

What does this passage
prompt me to pray to God?

_____

_____

LUKE 24:13-35

↻ _____

_____

← _____

_____

↑ _____

_____

↓ _____

_____

_____

→ _____

_____

↔ _____

_____

↰ _____

_____

_____

Jesus didn't rise from the dead and immediately ascend back to heaven. He appeared to numerous witnesses who would testify to His bodily resurrection from the dead. Many who saw Jesus alive were those who knew Him best, yet even they were prone to doubt that He was actually the Messiah until they saw with their own eyes. He also appeared to two travelers as they were discussing the rumors swirling around Jesus' death and resurrection. Jesus joined them and did something interesting—He took the writings of Moses and the prophets and showed them how everything about God's story pointed forward to the events that had happened in Jerusalem over the last several days. In many ways, Jesus did for these travelers what you're experiencing through this devotional. You can now see how all the Bible fits together to tell the single story of God's plan to save sinners and fix the world through Jesus Christ.

LUKE 24:36-53

The disciples were witnesses to Jesus life, death, and resurrection. The word "witness" is often used to describe someone who saw a crime or an accident. A witness testifies to an officer or jury about what he's seen or heard. We can also witness times of great joy—like a wedding or the birth of a baby. The first-hand knowledge that a person gains, not from simply hearing about an event, but seeing and experiencing it, puts them in a position to tell others what has happened. Jesus claimed that the disciples would serve as His witnesses for the rest of their lives. As He promised, the Holy Spirit was sent and would go with them, giving power to take the good news of salvation to the nations. Those who responded to their message were saved, and then sent out into the world as witnesses themselves.

JOHN 21:15-19

↻ _____

_____

_____

← _____

_____

_____

↑ _____

_____

_____

↓ _____

_____

_____

_____

→ _____

_____

_____

↔ _____

_____

_____

↰ _____

_____

_____

Peter messed up big time. He had trusted Jesus and experienced amazing things while following Him, but he also made some serious mistakes. Jesus even called him Satan—wow! At the end of Jesus' life, Peter had promised that he would never abandon his Master, even if that meant accompanying Him to the cross. Peter broke this promise and denied even knowing Jesus. But these failures were not the final verdict on Peter's life. Jesus, following His resurrection, appeared to Peter and reassured him of His love. Peter's three denials were matched by the three questions Jesus asked. Jesus had every right to drag up Peter's words and remind him of all the promises he had broken in the past. Jesus didn't—instead, He offered reassurance and gave Peter a mission to care for God's people. Peter's life provides hope that everyone has purpose in God's kingdom, even those who have made major mistakes.

1 CORINTHIANS 15:1-19

Paul reminded the church of the core of the good news. Certainly, there's more he told the church, but the heart of what he preached, and what all Christians are to believe, is the truth of Jesus' life, death, burial, and resurrection. Apparently, some in the church were denying the resurrection, claiming that those who died would not be resurrected one day. Paul countered this teaching, saying that all those with faith in Jesus would be raised just like Him. Jesus' resurrection proves that He defeated death on behalf of His people, and we will never experience the sting of eternal death. The empty tomb shouts Jesus' victory over Satan, sin, and death. Paul emphasized its importance with this bold idea—if we take out the resurrection, what we have is no longer the Christian faith.

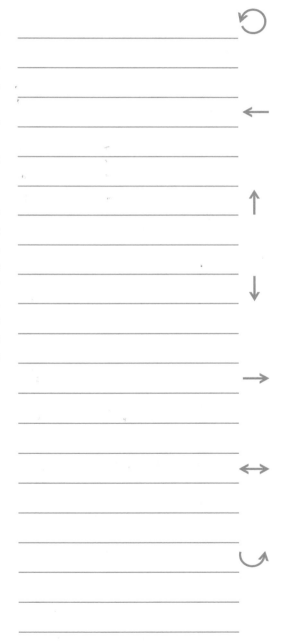

CHAPTER 8//CHURCH

The church resulted from God's mission to save sinners. Throughout the Old Testament, when we read of God's people, we were referring to the nation of Israel. This one nation received God's love and grace in a unique way as He prepared for the coming of Jesus. But salvation was not only available to Israelites; God continually held out the offer of salvation to all nations and willingly brought outsiders in to be part of His people.

This pattern continues in the New Testament. Jesus began His earthly mission by seeking out the Jews, the descendants of the nation of Israel, and inviting them to follow Him in faith. Most rejected Him.

After His resurrection, Jesus commissioned His followers to take the good news to all the nations. They reflected God's image and declared His message throughout the entire world. All who have responded to this message, regardless of ethnicity, age, or background, have been gathered into God's church. The church is comprised of all people—throughout all time and from every place around the world—who have trusted Jesus in faith. And one day all these will gather around the throne of God to proclaim His glory forever. For now, thousands upon thousands of churches, made up of local believers, meet together to worship God, learn from the Scriptures, love one another, grow in obedience to God's commands, and demonstrate God's glory to others.

The next chapter in God's story tells of the birth of the church. You may have been to a church at some point in your life, or you may be an active part of one right now. Some churches are so large you may feel like just a face in a crowd, whereas at some smaller churches everybody knows everybody. The diversity of the church shows up in service styles, the makeup of the congregation, and many other factors. But while the story of each church varies, all share a common story—the story of God. Every church, whether it's existed for decades or is just beginning, testifies to the faithfulness of God to continue saving sinners. He's been writing the story of the local church since the creation of the world.

MATTHEW 28:18-20

The twelve disciples were not the only followers of Jesus, but following His resurrection, Jesus gave these first followers a commission to make more disciples by a three-part process. First, they were to prioritize disciple-making as they went out into the world. Some were sent as missionaries to foreign nations, but all of the disciples were to make disciples as they went about their lives. Second, they were to baptize those who would come to faith in Jesus. Finally, they were to invest in teaching these individuals to obey Jesus in all things. This was a big mission, but Jesus provided hope that they could be faithful in their task. Jesus reminded them of His authority—He held the right to command His followers to make disciples. Then He promised He would go with them as they obeyed. They were not left alone, because the Holy Spirit would fill them with the power to make this massive mission possible.

What does this passage say?

What did this passage mean to its original audience?

What does this passage tell us about God?

What does this passage tell us about man?

What does this passage demand of me?

How does this passage change the way I relate to people?

What does this passage prompt me to pray to God?

ACTS 2:14-41

↺ _____
_____
_____

← _____
_____

↑ _____
_____

↓ _____
_____

→ _____
_____
_____

↔ _____
_____

↪ _____
_____
_____

Jesus charged His disciples to go on mission, then told them to wait until He sent the Holy Spirit. The Spirit's arrival in Acts 2 filled the first followers with power and passion to take the gospel from Jerusalem to Judea and Samaria and to the ends of the earth. Immediately, Peter explained the good news of Jesus to all those who would listen. Peter's sermon reminded His hearers that everything happening was just as God had planned. The death of Jesus, His resurrection, and now the sending of the Spirit was evidence that God's plan to save sinners and fix the world was being carried out. Jesus is both Lord and Christ, a fact that is visibly verified by His victory over death. Those who believe need simply to repent of their sins and follow Jesus in obedience, including baptism. Many thousands respond in faith, proving that God's mission did not end when Jesus died. He will continue His work through the faithful witness of His disciples.

ACTS 2:42-47

Luke, the author of the book of Acts, provided a number of glimpses into the life of the early church. The first church in Jerusalem was made up of those who came to faith in Jesus through the work of the disciples. As they gathered together regularly to hear from God's Word, to pray, and to fellowship with one another, God did astounding things among them. They experienced His power through many miracles, and God continued to save people and add them to the church. These early Christians actively loved and served one another by providing for those in need. The relationships in the church extend far deeper and are more profound than friendships that can be found in the world. The church is united by a common faith in Jesus and exists, not solely for the people themselves, but in order to worship the One who provided this great salvation.

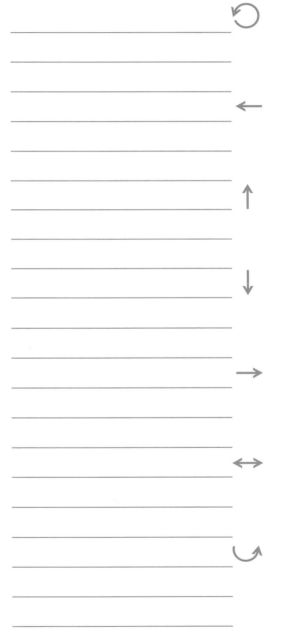

ACTS 5:12-42

The disciples faced the same type of persecution Jesus experienced. The rulers of the day didn't take kindly to these men and women who wouldn't stop talking about the man who was crucified—the One they claimed came back to life, and who they professed to be the rightful King of the world. These disciples not only preached about Jesus, but they also performed miracles in His name. The leaders tried to stop this movement by locking the disciples in prison, but God's mission could not be stopped. A God who displays His might and authority by conquering death will not be stopped by prison bars. In spite of the danger, the disciples took every opportunity to speak of Jesus. When they suffered, they found joy in the fact that God counted them worthy to suffer for His mission. They were driven by the conviction that God's mission was more important than their lives, and they would stop at nothing to see the good news spread.

2 CORINTHIANS 5:16-21

Jesus makes it possible for enemies of God to be brought back into right relationship with Him. Jesus drank the full cup of God's wrath for sin, giving the righteous life that He lived to sinners. Those who are reconciled are, in turn, to give our lives to see others made right with God. We should implore, or beg, other sinners to turn away from the momentary pleasures of sin and to pursue the eternal joys of Jesus. Everyone who experiences God's saving work receives this mission of reconciliation. Some will fulfill their task by becoming preachers or missionaries, and others will do so by sharing the gospel with their neighbors, friends, classmates, or coworkers. God positions all His people around others who need to know the hope Jesus brings. It's our mission to share that good news and trust God to bring salvation.

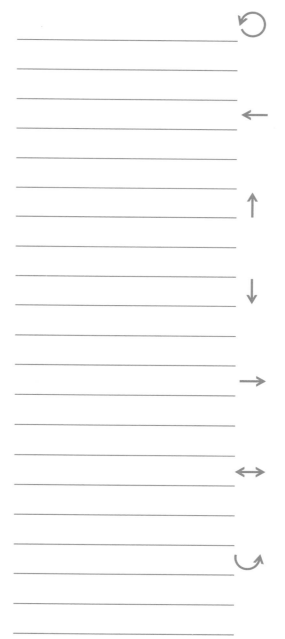

ACTS 7:54–8:3

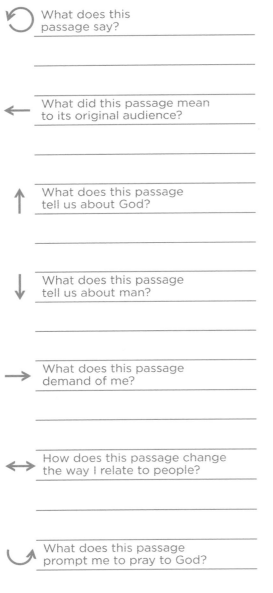

What does this
passage say?

What did this passage mean
to its original audience?

What does this passage
tell us about God?

What does this passage
tell us about man?

What does this passage
demand of me?

How does this passage change
the way I relate to people?

What does this passage
prompt me to pray to God?

God formed a unique plan to scatter His disciples. He intended for His followers to take the gospel message to the nations, but to this point, the church remained centered in Jerusalem. Stephen's death changed that. Followers of Jesus left Jerusalem because of the hatred they experienced and began to make their homes in adjacent regions and countries. Because His Spirit was in them, God went with these men and women, and the message of the gospel was carried into each new area. They no longer required a temple to worship because their bodies had become temples of God. They could worship wherever they went, and they could invite others to join with them in worship of the one true God. People from all nations, not just Israel, could now hear about Jesus, respond in faith, and gather together in the local church. God's mission was on the move.

ACTS 9:1-22

The first mention of Paul's name appeared during the story of Stephen's death. Paul, also known as Saul, was an intense persecutor of the church, even approving of the murder of many Christians. God took His most vocal opponent and turned Him into His most effective missionary. The remainder of the book of Acts and much of the New Testament tell the stories of Paul's mission work and the churches he started along the way. Thirteen of the letters he wrote are included in our Bible and continue to provide encouragement and instruction for the church today. God saved Paul in a most extraordinary way and immediately sent him on mission. The one who spoke in opposition to Jesus was transformed. Paul began joyfully sharing the good news that the man he once opposed, Jesus, is in fact the true God and the one all people owe allegiance.

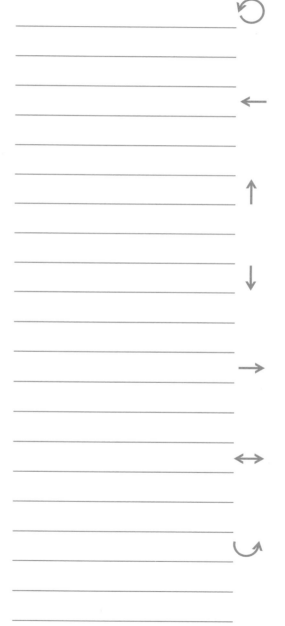

ACTS 11:1-18

↻ _____

_____

_____

← _____

_____

_____

↑ _____

_____

_____

↓ _____

_____

_____

→ _____

_____

_____

↔ _____

_____

_____

↪ _____

_____

_____

Up to this point, the majority of the Bible has focused on God's chosen people, the nation of Israel. Though a majority of them failed to trust in Jesus, they were the focus of God's work through Jesus and through the disciples. The Spirit of God and the salvation He offers is never confined to a certain nation, however. Non-Jews, also known as Gentiles, heard the message of salvation as Jesus' followers were scattered throughout the world. Amazingly, God was gracious to save them as well! For a time, the church debated whether or not God was actually willing to save non-Jews, but it's clear that this is exactly what He was doing. They received the Spirit of God, trusted Him in faith, and were baptized just the same. The church grew from a small band of disciples hiding in an upper room to a worldwide movement of people from every nation, just as God always intended.

ACTS 13

The remainder of the book of Acts is filled with stories of the church's expansion, which happened primarily because of the missionary work of men like Paul, Peter, and Barnabas. The church officially recognized God's saving work among the Gentiles and began to actively commission God's people to go to the nations to preach the gospel and plant churches. This work encountered a lot of difficulty, but it was destined all along to succeed. No one, not even Satan, can stop the advance of the church, because God has always been intent on seeing the earth filled with those who reflect His image. The book of Acts shows that He is doing just that. You, and the church you attend, are a continuation of this work which Jesus began long ago. He is still on mission to save sinners and gather them in local churches, from the high-rises of New York City to the jungles of Peru. Each of these churches can trace its origin back to these first missionaries and their faithful work.

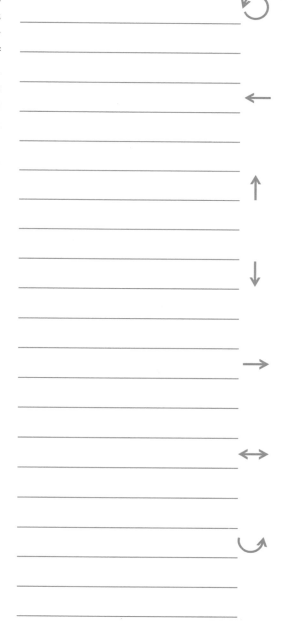

REVELATION 7:9-12

The book of Revelation contains John's vision of God's final victory over Satan, sin, and death, and His eternal rule in heaven. John saw a coming day when the promise God made to Abraham would come true—a large multitude, numbering like the stars in the heavens or the sand on the seashore, gathered around the throne to offer praise to God. Among this number are those God saved from every tribe, tongue, and nation on earth. There will be a day when the mission of God is complete, and the salvation of sinners throughout the world will be accomplished. This vast assortment of worshipers will receive the blessings that come to all those who are, by faith in Jesus, heirs of the promise made to Abraham. You've probably heard the children's song that tells of Jesus' love for all the little children of the world— whether they are red or yellow, black or white. Who knows whether or not we will sing this song in heaven, but we will certainly experience the truth of those words.

ROMANS 12

The first 11 chapters of the book of Romans contain the most extended discussion of the gospel message found in the Paul's writings. In chapter 12, he transitioned to a description of the life of a follower of Jesus. This was Paul's normal pattern in his letters. First, he summarized the good news, then he explained how that good news should change our lives. This order is important. Christians do not strive to obey God in order to be saved, but because they are saved. As Paul wrote here, they offered their lives as an act of worship to God. Everything they did was a response to the greatness of God—it showed how much He is worth. Worship isn't just what we do when we gather with the church to sing, it is every decision we make, every thought we think, every act we perform. We worship by reflecting God's image and showing His greatness in the ways we live each day.

What does this passage say?

What did this passage mean to its original audience?

What does this passage tell us about God?

What does this passage tell us about man?

What does this passage demand of me?

How does this passage change the way I relate to people?

What does this passage prompt me to pray to God?

1 CORINTHIANS 9:24-27

↻ _____
_____
_____
← _____
_____
_____
↑ _____
_____
_____
↓ _____
_____
_____
→ _____
_____
_____
↔ _____
_____
_____
↪ _____
_____
_____

The fact that we don't earn our salvation does not mean our actions aren't important. The very fact that God loved us so much that He sent Jesus to pay the price for our sins should actually make us more passionate to obey Him. Paul compared the Christian life to a race and challenged everyone to strive for the prize of faithfulness to God. Like athletes, this race will require great self-control. Any athlete who wants to win will have to watch what he or she eats and consistently train in order to operate at maximum potential. In the same way, Christians who want to be faithful will deny themselves the sinful cravings their hearts once desired, and by the power of the Holy Spirit, they will discipline themselves to say *no* to sin and *yes* to God every day. This type of self-control is key to living the life we were meant to live.

1 CORINTHIANS 12

God gives His people gifts that allow them to reflect His image in unique ways. The church is like a human body with various members having responsibilities that make the church healthy and effective. The key is for all church members to use the gifts given by God to serve one another in love. There are various lists of gifts throughout the New Testament. These serve as examples, but the lists are not meant to describe every single way someone might serve the church. However, we can be certain that every Christian, filled with the Holy Spirit, is given a gift to build up the church and help fulfill its mission. Paul cautioned against comparing your gift to that of someone else. He reminded the church that God knows what He is doing. He gives gifts as He desires. It's not up to us to question God's wisdom, but simply to use what we've been given to fulfill the mission He puts before each of us.

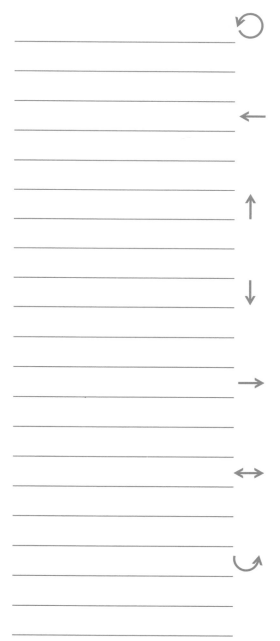

1 CORINTHIANS 13

↺ _____

_____

_____

← _____

_____

_____

_____

↑ _____

_____

_____

↓ _____

_____

_____

→ _____

_____

_____

_____

↔ _____

_____

_____

↪ _____

_____

_____

Love is at the very center of the Christian life, and this has always been true. In fact, all the Old Testament law can be summarized as a command to love—God above all else, and others who are made in His image. The church is no different. We are a people united in a common love for God and called to a sacrificial love for one another. Paul made it clear that God empowers His people to do all sorts of amazing things, but any action that is not motivated by love is useless—God has always been most concerned with the heart behind our actions. He can use anyone or anything to accomplish His purposes, and He doesn't have to use any one of us. He doesn't need our actions—He wants our hearts. The fact that He is willing to use us in His mission is a sheer privilege. This should compel us to love Him and, in turn, love the people He's created.

EPHESIANS 5:22-33

Paul compared the love of Jesus for His people to the love a husband should have for his wife. In fact, God created marriage to show the world how He loves His people. Sadly, in a broken world, marriages are often poor reflections of God's love. The tragedy of divorce shows that people don't love like God does. The fact that people are difficult to love should come as no surprise. We're all sinful, which is why God created marriage to put His love on display. Jesus loves His people in spite of our sin. He gave His life to show His love even though we've continually turned our backs on Him to pursue other loves. The type of love God shows isn't just the feeling of affection—it's a commitment based on His promises. He pledged His love to His people, and He will always be faithful to His promises. When husbands and wives love one another in this way, they show the world what God is like.

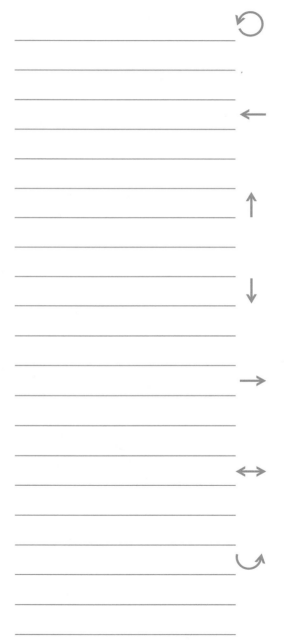

2 CORINTHIANS 4:7-18

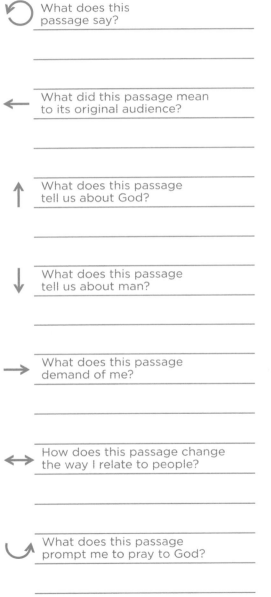

What does this passage say?

What did this passage mean to its original audience?

What does this passage tell us about God?

What does this passage tell us about man?

What does this passage demand of me?

How does this passage change the way I relate to people?

What does this passage prompt me to pray to God?

Faithfulness to God's mission is not always easy, and it can be a real challenge to reflect His image while living in bodies broken by sin. We get tired, grow old, and wear down—this is a result of sin's curse. Our bodies are like jars of clay which are easily broken and shattered. Paul's life was a picture of this reality. He experienced the joy of planting churches and seeing many come to faith. He also felt the agony of persecution. He knew the pain of following God in a broken world, but he looked beyond the immediate pain, comparing his temporary suffering to the future joy that awaits all God's people. In the big picture, suffering in this life is insignificant compared to our eternal blessings. Paul said that the future is so great, so full of glory, that no amount of human sadness and suffering even compares.

GALATIANS 5:16–6:10

God's people live by the power of His Spirit. The Holy Spirit fills believers and gives us grace to live distinctly from those who don't know Jesus. The fruit of the sinful life is seen in all sorts of rebellious behavior, but the fruit of God's Spirit produces love, joy, peace, patience, kindness, goodness, faithfulness, gentleness, and self-control. These attitudes and behaviors are like fruit on a tree—we can look at people's actions, either bad or good, and know whether they are filled by God's Spirit or not. Godly fruit allows a person to live in loving relationships with other people, reflecting the love God demonstrates to us. This type of love is the defining mark of God's church, as diverse people show love for one another because we are united by a common love for God.

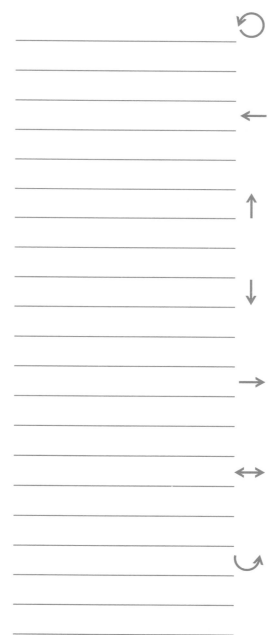

EPHESIANS 2:11-22

↻ _____

_____

_____

← _____

_____

_____

↑ _____

_____

↓ _____

_____

_____

→ _____

_____

↔ _____

_____

↺ _____

_____

_____

Unity is a defining mark of the church that stands out in this passage. Paul reminded Gentile believers that they were, at one time, not only cut off from God because of their sin, they were cut off from God's people as well. They were outsiders to God's law, the sacrificial system and the temple, but Jesus' death brought them into right relationship with God, allowing them to join the family of God. Together, Jews and Gentiles alike are united as the people of God and members of the church. Paul then used an image familiar to the nation of Israel when he described their unity as a new temple— one not made with human hands, but built by the hand of God. Each person who comes to faith in Jesus is like a new stone added to God's temple. In this way, Gentiles, who were once outsiders, are now participants in the life of the temple as they worship Him in the church.

EPHESIANS 4:1-16

The church gathers in unity because all those who make up the church are adopted into the same family—because there is one God, there is one family of God. This doesn't mean that everyone who comes to a church building each week is part of God's family. Many who participate in weekly gatherings do not truly know Jesus, and there are many reasons why these people attend. The ones who truly belong to the church are those who have trusted Jesus and have committed their lives to reflecting His image in the world. God appoints leaders who are given the task of equipping the church for this work, so that each individual Christian can grow in the way God intends. Christians who commit themselves to the church join with other believers in the work of becoming more and more like Jesus.

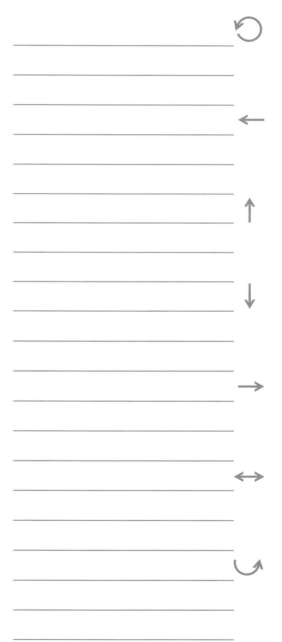

1 PETER 5:1-11

↺ _____
_____
_____
← _____
_____
_____
↑ _____
_____
_____
↓ _____
_____
_____
→ _____
_____
_____
↔ _____
_____
↪ _____
_____
_____

The leaders of the church are meant to be a reflection of the way God leads His people. We've already seen how Jesus used the image of a shepherd to communicate the way He loves and leads His sheep. In the same way, pastors are to act like shepherds for the church. They work to lead sheep to spiritual food, care for them when they are hurt, and protect them from harm. These leaders are not meant to lead in their own human strength, but they are to be exemplary in the ways they live, constantly submitting to God's guidance. Throughout His story, God has always used human leaders to care for His people. Some led well and others were terrible failures. What separates a great leader from a bad one is his love for God and obedience to God's leadership. A church blessed by godly pastors should give thanks to God for leaders who love them and point them to God's shepherding care.

COLOSSIANS 3:1-17

Paul compared the process of reflecting the image of God to changing clothes. A person wearing dirty clothes needs simply to take off the old clothes and put on new, clean clothes. The old clothes represent our former life of sin. We know all of our sin—past, present, and future—has been forgiven by Jesus, and we now stand before God pure and holy. But we still sin. We fail to reflect God's image in all the ways we should. For the rest of our lives, we will continually take off the old clothes, those actions that were regular parts of our lives before we came to faith in Jesus. The process of putting off sin is known as repentance. It's what we did when we first began to follow Jesus—when we admitted our sin and asked God to give us the power to turn from it. We then put on our new clothes, the actions that define a follower of Jesus. God's power at work in our hearts will result in these new actions and will show that we are truly God's children.

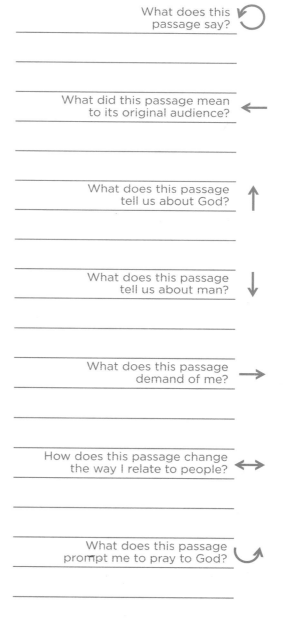

What does this passage say?

What did this passage mean to its original audience?

What does this passage tell us about God?

What does this passage tell us about man?

What does this passage demand of me?

How does this passage change the way I relate to people?

What does this passage prompt me to pray to God?

1 THESSALONIANS 4:1-12

Do you ever hear big Christian words and tune them out because you don't really know what they mean? Sanctification may be one of those words, but it holds an important truth for the Christian life. Sanctification is the process of putting off sin and putting on holiness. Throughout the Old Testament, God took common items and set them apart for use in worship in the temple. A table or a kitchen utensil would be cleansed and used by the High Priest while offering sacrifices. Once the item was used in this way, it was holy and would not return to common use. In the same way, Paul said that believers in Jesus are set apart for a holy life and mission. Faith in Jesus has made us holy, and our lives should reflect this newfound identity. We should never return to lives of unholy living. A holy life clearly sets God's people apart from the world, not so we can take pride in how good we are, but so the world can see the transformation that faith in Jesus brings.

1 TIMOTHY 4:6-16

Timothy pastored a young church in Ephesus. A long-time friend of Paul, Timothy followed Paul's example of godly living and gospel work and was given the task of leading God's people in a church filled with challenging issues. Timothy might have been tempted to doubt his ability or calling, so Paul reminded him that his confidence should come from God and not from what others think. In fact, Timothy was responsible for setting the pace for others, even those who were older than him, by faithfully living in obedience to God. This work would not be easy, so Timothy needed to keep a close watch on his life, putting off sin and pursuing godliness. He also needed to hold firm to the truth of the gospel, refusing to give in to false teaching that would undermine the work of Jesus. Timothy challenges believers, particularly young Christians, to pursue godliness in all things and to trust God to use us to make a difference in His church.

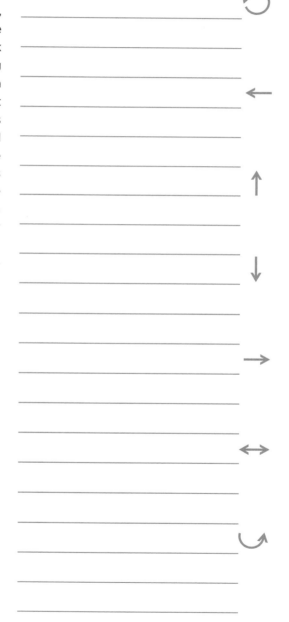

1 TIMOTHY 6:1-10

↻ _____
_____
_____

← _____
_____
_____

↑ _____
_____

↓ _____
_____
_____

→ _____
_____
_____
_____

↔ _____
_____
_____

↺ _____
_____
_____

The world of Paul's day was very different from ours in many ways, but there are common factors that shape life in a fallen world regardless of when or where a person lives. People often worry about the future and feel unsatisfied with the lives they've been given. We think that we would be happy and fulfilled, if we only had a little more money, a certain relationship, or were the star of the team. Paul challenged Timothy to refuse this perspective and to live a life marked by contentment. A Christian has already experienced the best there is this side of heaven—we've been saved by grace through faith in Jesus Christ, and nothing can take this salvation away. We are eternally secure in Jesus' love, so we can be content with whatever comes in this life. Whether we have a little or a lot, whether we are young or old, whether we feel important or feel like no one cares, we can relax and enjoy the grace of God we've been given.

1 TIMOTHY 6:11-21

Jesus makes obedience possible and sets the example for how to live a faithful life to the final breath. At the outset of His ministry, Satan tempted Jesus to walk a different path to greatness than the one that led to the cross. At the end of His life, Pilate asked Jesus if He claimed to be God. Had Jesus denied that He was God's Son, He likely would have avoided execution. Jesus looked death in the face and confronted it head-on because of His faith in the promises of the Father. He knew that His death would save sinners, and that God would raise Him again on the third day. This same type of faith in the promise of God to raise believers on the last day provides the confidence we need to walk in faithfulness, even when we suffer for doing what is right.

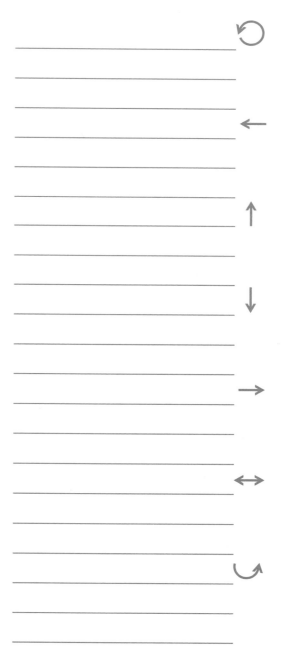

2 TIMOTHY 3:10-17

What does this
passage say?

_____

_____

What did this passage mean
to its original audience?

_____

_____

What does this passage
tell us about God?

_____

_____

What does this passage
tell us about man?

_____

_____

What does this passage
demand of me?

_____

_____

How does this passage change
the way I relate to people?

_____

_____

What does this passage
prompt me to pray to God?

_____

_____

God reveals Himself by speaking. Think about it. There would be no way for us to know any details about God if He didn't tell us who He is and what He came to do. The Bible records the very words of God given to help us understand His character, our sin, and the work of Jesus. Paul said that every word in the Bible is God-breathed, meaning that it came straight from Him to us, and it is perfect. Scripture teaches us how to follow God and corrects us when we don't. For many of us, the Bible may be one of the most underused gifts we've ever received. We probably have a copy, or many copies, of God's Word, but we often fail to read the Bible and apply it to our lives. Hopefully, the Seven Arrows method has given you confidence to read God's Word as you've learned to understand and apply the Bible to your life. Every time we open the Bible, we receive one of God's greatest gifts, and it changes our lives.

PHILEMON 1

The power of the good news allows people who are vastly different to link arms in unity. Paul wrote this short letter to Philemon concerning one of his slaves, Onesimus, who converted to Christianity after escaping from slavery. Paul met Onesimus, and the two became friends and co-workers. Paul asked Philemon to do the unthinkable—to receive Onesimus back, not only without consequences for escaping, but treating him like a fellow brother. Because he had come to faith in Jesus, he was a fellow brother with Paul and Philemon in God's family. Paul demonstrated his love for Onesimus by telling Philemon that he would pay back anything Onesimus owed for his wrongdoing. This type of love is only made possible by the gospel of Jesus. Regardless of who people are, what they've done, or how different they may be from us, we can treat all believers like fellow brothers and sisters when God adopts us into His family.

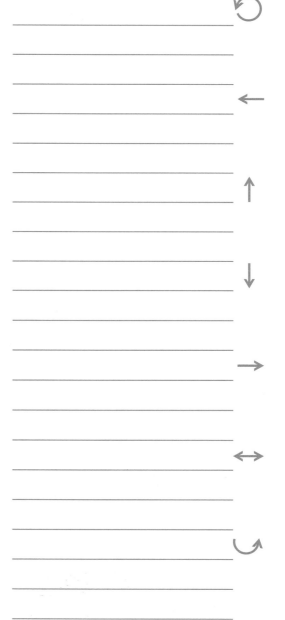

HEBREWS 10:19-25

↻ _____
_____
_____
← _____
_____
_____
↑ _____
_____
↓ _____
_____
→ _____
_____
↔ _____
_____
↻ _____
_____
_____

The book of Hebrews overflows with examples illustrating how Jesus fulfills the promises and plans of God revealed in the Old Testament. We've already seen numerous examples showing Jesus is better than Israel's leaders, the sacrifices, and even the temple. Near the end of the book, the writer shifted to practical application for how these ideas should impact our lives. Here he wrote that we should have confidence to draw near in worship since, through Jesus, our sins have been forgiven. We should not neglect to join with others in worship, because the ability to approach God is a privilege we do not deserve. You've probably heard others tell you about the importance of church, but you might underestimate just how important it really is. We gather regularly with God's people in the church to continue working together to grow in our love for God and for one another.

HEBREWS 11

This chapter, often called "The Hall of Fame of Faith," recounts the lives of people who reflected extraordinary faith. You've read the stories of many of these men and women throughout this devotional. Though the details differ, God gave each of them a promise, and they respond by trusting Him. The faith of some shaped nations and won wars. Others on the list suffered for their faith—in fact, some of their names aren't even mentioned and only God knows who they are. God sees the faith of His people and takes notice. It's faith that allows us access to God's grace, which is how we become Christians in the first place. Faith is also the fuel that drives us to live every day for Christ. In other words, we come to Jesus by faith and we live in obedience by faith. The greatest thing that could be said of any of us at the end of our lives is that we were men or women of great faith.

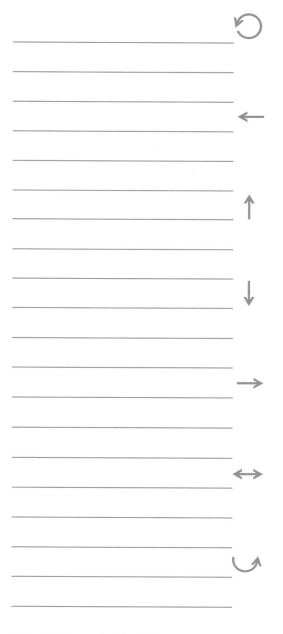

2 TIMOTHY 2:1-13

↺ _____

_____

← _____

_____

_____

↑ _____

_____

↓ _____

_____

→ _____

_____

↔ _____

_____

↪ _____

_____

Suffering is a common theme in the New Testament. Followers of Jesus were often persecuted for their faith, especially leaders like Paul and Timothy. Paul led the way for missions and church planting in the first century, and he also suffered in unimaginable ways during his travels. Paul didn't tell young Timothy to simply follow his example in suffering well. Instead, he pointed his attention back to Jesus, who is the prime example of suffering. He is worth the lives of His followers, and Paul reminded Timothy that life and death are not what's truly important. What matters most is the fact that God promises eternal salvation to His people, and God never breaks His promises, even when we break ours. He is always faithful, so even if this life brings suffering and pain, we can trust that God will grant us new bodies in a restored world where we will worship Him forever.

JAMES 1:19-27

James loaded his book with practical wisdom about how God's people should live, including topics such as favoritism between those in the church and the consequences of our words. Writing to people who had already professed faith in Jesus, he pointed to truth that they can now obey since they've been given a new heart and have God's Spirit living within them. The core of James' challenge boils down to believers obeying God, particularly the things He tells them to do through Scripture. He compared the Bible to a mirror because it reveals our sin and our need for Jesus. The more we hold the Bible up to our lives, the better we're able to see what we actually look like, then we can make necessary changes. Because our sin is so deep and affects so many areas of our lives, we must do this daily, allowing God to point out our sin. In fact, He'll often point out the same sin over and over again, and we'll have to continually strive to apply the truth He reveals to bring the change we so desperately need.

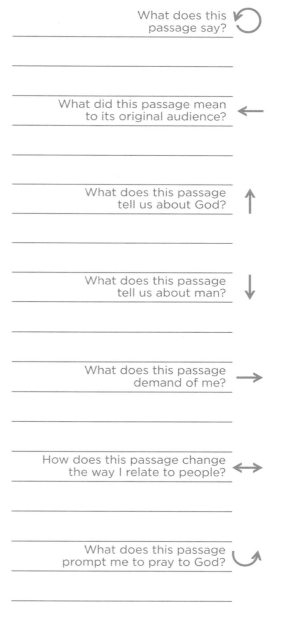

What does this passage say?

What did this passage mean to its original audience?

What does this passage tell us about God?

What does this passage tell us about man?

What does this passage demand of me?

How does this passage change the way I relate to people?

What does this passage prompt me to pray to God?

1 PETER 2:1-12

↺ _____

_____

_____

← _____

_____

_____

↑ _____

_____

_____

↓ _____

_____

_____

→ _____

_____

_____

↔ _____

_____

_____

↰ _____

_____

_____

Many of the words and concepts in this passage come straight from the Old Testament. Peter applied the ideas to the church showing that God was accomplishing His plan from the Old Testament, laying the foundation for God's saving work through Jesus. The church is not simply a place for God's people to gather, but is God's people united to be sent on mission. Their lives and their words are to testify to the world about the glory of God revealed through Christ. Evangelism, or the sharing of the good news, should overflow from the lives of everyone in the church, not just the church's pastors. Like the nation of Israel, others are meant to look at our lives and see the noticeable difference Jesus has made. We are then able share about the work of Jesus, inviting others to trust Him and be changed as well.

1 JOHN 3:11-24

The love Christians have for God and other people is a defining mark and makes us distinct from those who don't follow Jesus. The Old Testament law could be summarized by these two commands: love God and love others. The love we show others should be modeled after the love God demonstrated to us in Jesus. This love is more than a feeling of affection—all along, God's love has been a commitment to action. He said He loved us and acted for the good of those who were objects of His love— even when we were not lovable, and when love would cost Him greatly. The love we show others works the same way. We should love other people simply because that's what we're called to do as Christians. It should not be based on their loveliness, but on our commitment. And we should be willing to show love even when it's costly and when we get nothing in return. When we love people who are like us or who help us in some way, we are no different than the world. We show Christian love when we love the unlovable, and for no other reason than to be like Jesus.

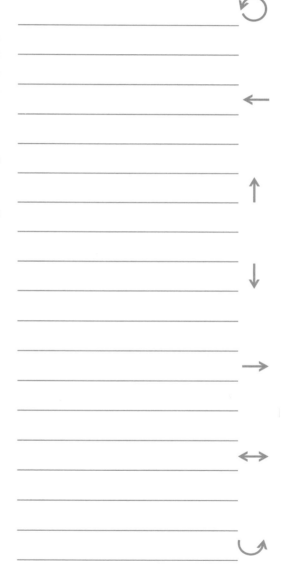

1 JOHN 5:1-5

↻ _____
_____
_____

← _____
_____
_____

↑ _____
_____
_____

↓ _____
_____
_____

→ _____
_____
_____

↔ _____
_____
_____

↪ _____
_____
_____

John said that you could recognize genuine followers of Jesus by their love for God and obedience to His commandments. As we've seen throughout this devotional, we're not striving to love God or keep His commandments so that we can earn His love. He already loves us and demonstrated the depth of that love through Jesus' sacrifice. Now that we're born of God and are His children, our hearts desire to please Him. It's a telltale mark of someone who has truly experienced the love of Jesus. It's impossible that we experience God's love in a transformational way, then turn around and live however we want. We obey because, as Christians, we desire to please God more than anything else. This doesn't mean we will always obey perfectly. At times, we will sin and fail, but God's people are quick to repent from sin, then commit ourselves once again to wholeheartedly obeying God.

JUDE 1:17-25

The Bible begins and ends with a glorious God. The world is wasting away as a result of human sin, and people continually attempt to undermine the work of the church and the spread of the gospel. Jude wrote that times were difficult, and they were only going to get worse. However, the church can't abandon its mission when life is tough. We must continue to obey God, live holy lives, and preach the message of Jesus in spite of the challenges we face. Our only hope to fulfill this task lies in the faithfulness of God. He promised to save His people and fix His broken world, and He will certainly do it. This is the story He's been writing for all time. Though our lives seem big and important, in reality we are only a small part in the grand story of God. We should recognize that what's most important isn't whether or not the various details of our lives play out the way we'd like. What's important is that we give our lives to God, allowing Him to do with us as He pleases.

CHAPTER 9//ETERNITY

God finishes what He starts. His plan to save sinners and fix the world leads to a final chapter when God accomplishes what He set out to do when His story began. God's story isn't like the story of our lives. Our stories have a beginning and an end—a day we're born and a day we die—and all sorts of things happen between these two days. We all have many happy moments—times we laugh with friends, win a big game, or get accepted to our dream school. We also have many sad moments. There will be times when we lose someone we love, and times when our friends hurt us deeply. From our perspective, many things about life will not make sense, and certain chapters of our stories may seem random and unclear.

God's story does have a lot in common with ours (He's certainly experienced joys and sorrows), but God doesn't have a beginning or an end like we do. He is eternal, meaning He has always existed and will exist forever. And one huge difference between God's experience and ours is that He's the One writing the story. He knows how all of the various parts of our story—the good and the bad—are going to come together to show off His glory.

That's exactly what He's doing with all the details of the world we experience every day. He's working to fill the earth with His glory. He wants everyone, everywhere to know how great He is. The final chapter of God's story will prove His greatness once and for all as Jesus returns and brings an end to the world as we know it. He's going to claim all of His people, living and dead, and remake the world as the perfect creation He intended from the beginning. He will prove His permanent defeat of Satan, sin, and death, and those who have trusted Jesus will live eternally, worshiping and serving Him in this new world. He will save sinners and fix the world—forever!

We now know the beginning and the end of God's story, as told in the pages of Scripture. It's amazing that God has been so kind to tell us all these details. We might wonder why things happen like they do in the story of our lives, but we never have to wonder or worry about what's happening in God's story. He's told us what will happen, and as we've seen throughout the Bible, God always stays true to His word.

2 PETER 3:1-13

The churches in the Bible hoped that Jesus would return during their lives. He didn't, and believers began to wonder why. Peter reminded the church that a delay in Jesus' return is for a purpose—more and more people are given a chance to repent. Some people will mock Christians, thinking that, because Jesus hasn't returned yet, He never will. The church shouldn't lose heart. Jesus will return as He's said, and when He does, He is going to remake the world. All that is broken about our current world will be made whole—people will no longer sin and the world will no longer be broken by sin. This new world will be filled with the glory of God and everyone will clearly know that He is worthy of praise.

What does this passage say?

What did this passage mean to its original audience?

What does this passage tell us about God?

What does this passage tell us about man?

What does this passage demand of me?

How does this passage change the way I relate to people?

What does this passage prompt me to pray to God?

LUKE 12:35-48

🔄 _____

_____

_____

← _____

_____

↑ _____

_____

↓ _____

_____

→ _____

_____

↔ _____

_____

↰ _____

_____

_____

God has already written the story, but He alone knows when the final chapter will play out. Jesus prepared His disciples, knowing that no one will be able to predict His return. It will be like a thief, who comes at night when no one is looking. Christians can be tempted to become lazy when He doesn't come back quickly, and Jesus compares this with a servant's awaiting his master's return. At first the servant is prompt and attentive to every detail, knowing that the master could return at any time. Of course, he wants everything in order when that time comes. If the master is delayed, the servant might fall asleep or simply lose focus on the master's needs. When the master returns, the servant will be caught off guard. Jesus cautions His followers to be attentive and diligent while He is away. We aren't simply to sit around and bide time. Instead, we should focus on the mission He's given us, striving to invest our lives in work that matters. This active obedience is the mark of a Christian who understands what it means to be ready for Jesus' return.

LUKE 14:12-24

One of the most common images of heaven is the picture of a great banquet. God hosts this lavish party, and the guests are invited to enjoy the feast He provides. The most likely guests at the final banquet, the Jews, have largely rejected the invitation, so God invites others to the banquet in their place. Gentiles are now given a place of honor at the feast. Jesus instructed His early followers to go into every part of the world, inviting anyone who would come to join them at the party. Anyone who places faith in Jesus, whether Jew or Gentile, now receives the same invitation to come and feast. Down through the centuries, this invitation has been extended to people like us. We too can come to God's banquet when He returns and makes all things new. The final banquet will be like the greatest party you've ever attended, one with food and friends celebrating God's goodness together.

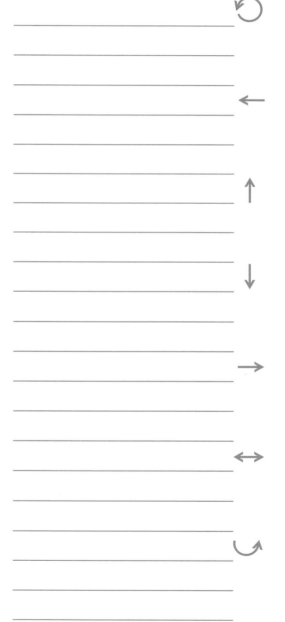

1 THESSALONIANS 4:13–5:11

The final chapter of God's story gives hope for those who place their faith in Jesus. We can trust that death will not have the final word—we will be raised with new life in Christ Jesus in a restored body living in a renewed world. Believers can also take comfort that any relatives or friends who have trusted in Jesus will experience the same eternal life. Those who have died, or to use Paul's language, those who have "fallen asleep," will rise to new life when Jesus returns. We should grieve when those we love die, but we should not lose hope. Though they are absent from us for a time in this world, they are together with God for all eternity, and we will see them again one day. We're not told all the details of our relationships with others in heaven, but we should be encouraged by the fact that everyone who has faith in Jesus will spend eternity forever in His presence.

REVELATION 1:1-8

The second coming of Jesus will be a time when everyone will see God's glory, both the saved and the unsaved. For those who chose to continue living in their sin, rejecting Jesus' offer of salvation, they will live with the consequences of their choice in hell. Because they have not trusted Jesus, the end will be filled with regret and pain—they will be separated forever from God's goodness and will experience His full wrath. The opposite experience awaits those who have trusted Jesus. We've seen and experienced God's glory, but never in the way we will experience Him in heaven. Because we will be free from sin and guilt, our perspectives will be perfectly clear as we are now fit to dwell in His presence in perfect holiness. We will also fully understand His story once and for all. He will prove that, just as He started the story, He's been faithful to complete it in a way that shows how glorious He actually is.

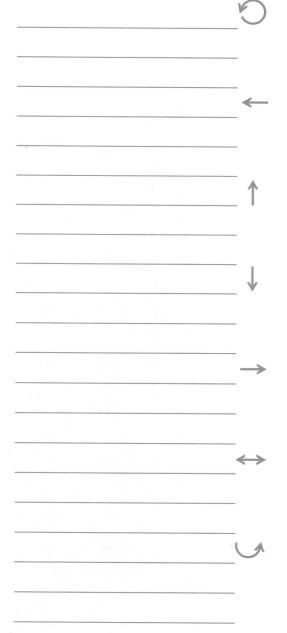

REVELATION 3:14-22

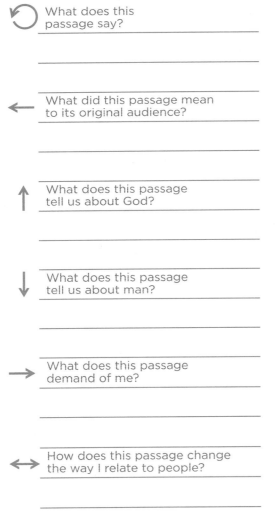

What does this passage say?

What did this passage mean to its original audience?

What does this passage tell us about God?

What does this passage tell us about man?

What does this passage demand of me?

How does this passage change the way I relate to people?

What does this passage prompt me to pray to God?

God gives a strict warning to seven churches in the book of Revelation. At one time each church followed Him with a vibrant faith, but because they'd fallen away in one way or another, God threatened to remove His presence from them. Remember back in the Old Testament when the nation of Israel would enter battle without the presence of God, and they would get crushed? The same is true for the church in the New Testament. Though the enemies are different, if God removes His presence from His people, they will fail. The key to the health of the church is its willingness to repent and return to the Lord. The picture given in Revelation is astounding. God stands outside the church knocking on the door, asking to be let in. The churches who hear Him knocking and humbly open the door are the ones He will fill with His power and presence. Churches today face the same issue. We must consistently repent and return to God, acknowledging our need for His continual presence, or we will be in jeopardy of going through the motions, but doing so without God.

REVELATION 5

There's a lot in the book of Revelation that is difficult to understand, but what's most important is abundantly clear—God wins! His story finishes just as He said it would, with Jesus as the hero. He's the Lamb who was slain, and who is worthy of all worship. John reminded us that this Lamb is not like any other sacrifice, but He's the One who was promised—from the tribe of Judah and who inherits the throne of David. Through His death and resurrection, He has defeated Satan, sin, and death, and now Jesus' victory is final. Our glimpse into this final chapter proves that heaven's focus is on God. He's the One worthy of praise and worship because His glory can now be clearly seen. No one but God could write the story of sinners saved and the broken world restored, and He's the only One capable of making it actually happen. That type of power and glory are worth the praise of all creation.

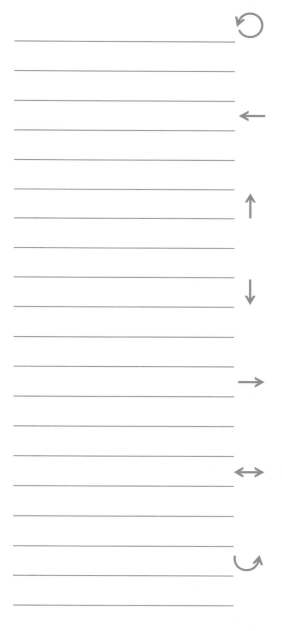

REVELATION 7:9-17

↺ _____
_____
_____
← _____
_____
_____
↑ _____
_____
_____
↓ _____
_____
_____
→ _____
_____
_____
↔ _____
_____
_____
↪ _____
_____
_____

In the new heaven and earth, God's mission to fill the earth with worship will be complete. It's always been His goal to save sinners from every corner of His world. The mission of the church is to take the gospel message to all people, and as we do, God is faithful to save those who trust in Jesus. The final chapter of God's story will not be written until this mission is complete. John's vision in Revelation shows us that, like every aspect of God's story, He will accomplish this mission as well. Around the throne of God, we see faithful people from every tribe, tongue, and nation who have experienced God's saving grace. The diversity of heaven shows that God's offer of salvation extends to all people, everywhere. The fact that God can save all sinners, not just some, proves the depth of His love for the image-bearers He's made.

REVELATION 21:1-8

Imagine a perfect world, free from all forms of pain, suffering, and sin. It's hard to imagine, right? We live in a world that is broken in every conceivable way. We see the implications of sin on a daily basis—in the news, in our schools, in our families, and in our own lives. Thankfully the part of God's story we're currently experiencing is not the end of the story. There's a better day coming. On that day, God will make all things new. He'll take all that has been broken by sin and fix it, including the people who bear His image as well as creation. Since the world will be free from sin, God will once again be able to dwell with His people, and this time there will be no need for sacrifices and temples. His presence will fill the earth and everyone will know that He alone is God. Joy will be the song of heaven as we see God's plan has come to fruition. For now, we live with unrelenting anticipation that God would come quickly and finish His story.

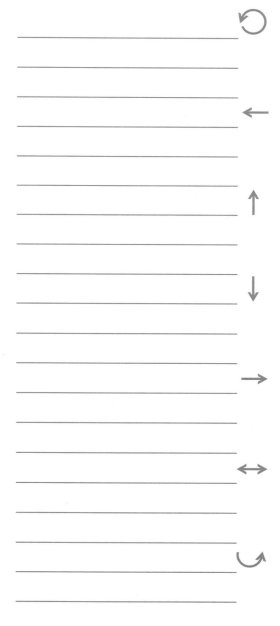

REVELATION 22:1-5

_____

_____

_____

_____

_____

_____

_____

_____

_____

_____

_____

_____

_____

_____

_____

John's vision ends with a scene that is a clear reminder of the garden He made when He first created the world. Rivers and trees picture the glory of the Creator. This new world is different in many ways, though. There will be no sun or moon, because all that's needed to light this world is the glory of God. There will also be no way for sin to mess up the new world—sin and Satan will be defeated forever, and they will no longer be able to tempt God's image-bearers to rebel. We're not told how many people will live in this world, but we know an abundance of perfected people will live in this perfected world. Like Adam and Eve, these worshipers are given a task—they will rule over God's creation and enjoy all that He's made. These faithful ones will inherit the glorious privilege of completing their mission of filling the earth with the glory of God. They will continue on this mission forever because the final chapter of God's story never ends.

NOTES

NOTES

NOTES

NOTES

A MAN HAD TWO DOGS.
THE ONE HE FED
GREW THE
BIGGEST.

WORSHIP
scripture
SOLITUDE
fasting

MINISTRY
prayer
COMMUNITY